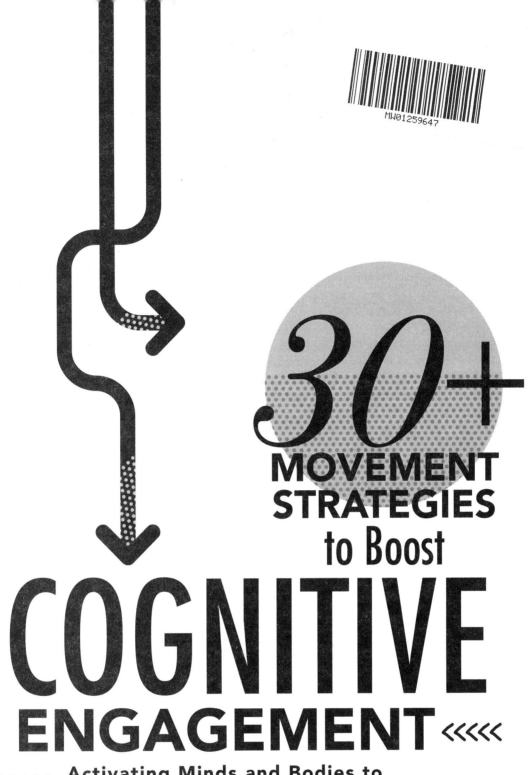

# 30+ MOVEMENT STRATEGIES to Boost

# COGNITIVE ENGAGEMENT «««

>>>>> Activating Minds and Bodies to Maximize Student Learning

## Rebecca Stobaugh

Solution Tree | Press

a division of
Solution Tree

555 North Morton Street
Bloomington, IN 47404
800.733.6786 (toll free) / 812.336.7700
FAX: 812.336.7790

email: info@SolutionTree.com
SolutionTree.com

Visit **go.SolutionTree.com/studentengagement** to download the free reproducibles in this book.

Printed in the United States of America

Library of Congress Cataloging-in-Publication Data

Names: Stobaugh, Rebecca, author.
Title: 30+ movement strategies to boost cognitive engagement : activating
   minds and bodies to maximize student learning / Rebecca Stobaugh.
Other titles: Thirty plus movement strategies to boost cognitive engagement
Description: Bloomington, IN : Solution Tree Press, [2022] | Includes
   bibliographical references and index.
Identifiers: LCCN 2022030048 (print) | LCCN 2022030049 (ebook)
ISBN 9781954631755 (paperback) | ISBN 9781954631762 (ebook)
Subjects: LCSH: Cognitive learning. | Movement, Psychology of. | Movement
   education. | Active learning. | Classroom environment.
Classification: LCC LB1062 .S786 2022  (print) | LCC LB1062  (ebook) | DDC
   370.15/23--dc23/eng/20220707
LC record available at https://lccn.loc.gov/2022030048
LC ebook record available at https://lccn.loc.gov/2022030049

---

**Solution Tree**
Jeffrey C. Jones, CEO
Edmund M. Ackerman, President

**Solution Tree Press**
*President and Publisher:* Douglas M. Rife
*Associate Publisher:* Sarah Payne-Mills
*Managing Production Editor:* Kendra Slayton
*Editorial Director:* Todd Brakke
*Art Director:* Rian Anderson
*Copy Chief:* Jessi Finn
*Production Editor:* Paige Duke
*Content Development Specialist:* Amy Rubenstein
*Copy Editor:* Madonna Evans
*Proofreader:* Sarah Ludwig
*Text Designer:* Julie Csizmadia
*Cover Designer:* Rian Anderson
*Associate Editor:* Sarah Ludwig
*Editorial Assistants:* Charlotte Jones and Elijah Oates

# Acknowledgments

Thank you to the K–12 teachers involved in developing the materials for this book. Courtney Lyons Biggs, Gracie Taylor, and Faith Coles assisted in both researching and describing the strategies profiled. They were key in giving feedback on how the book should be structured and lent a practical lens to the work.

I'd also like to thank those who contributed content area examples: Lauren Miller, Sophie Pemberton, Clare Cecil, Rebecca Fields, and Jennifer Webb. Thank you to Drs. Brooke Bartrug and Christy W. Bryce for sharing their expertise by recommending ways to differentiate the strategies to meet diverse learners.

Finally, I'm grateful to Keri Mosier and Will Perry, who provided a thorough review.

Solution Tree Press would like to thank the following reviewers:

Alexander Fangman
Principal
Summit View Academy
Independence, Kentucky

Rachel Swearengin
Fifth-Grade Teacher
Manchester Park Elementary School
Olathe, Kansas

Kelly Hilliard
Math Teacher
McQueen High School
Reno, Nevada

Ringnolda Jofee' Tremain
K-8 Principal
Trinity Leadership Arlington
Arlington, Texas

Tom Krawczewicz
Director of Educational Resources
DeMatha Catholic High School
Hyattsville, Maryland

Sheryl Walters
Instructional Design Lead
Calgary Academy
Calgary, Alberta

Visit **go.SolutionTree.com/studentengagement** to download the free reproducibles in this book.

# Table of Contents

*Reproducibles are in italics.*

# 4 Moving in Groups 47

# 5 Moving With Games 71

# About the Author

**Rebecca Stobaugh** is a professor at Western Kentucky University in Bowling Green, Kentucky, where she teaches assessment and unit-planning courses in the teacher education program. She also leads several teacher-induction cadres for regional districts and consults with school districts on critical thinking, assessment, technology integration, and other topics. Previously, she served as a middle and high school teacher and middle school principal. In 2004, she received the Social Studies Teacher of the Year Award from the Kentucky Council for the Social Studies.

Rebecca has authored several books, including *Assessing Critical Thinking in Elementary Schools*, *Assessing Critical Thinking in Middle and High Schools*, *Real-World Learning Framework for Secondary Schools*, *Real-World Learning Framework for Elementary Schools*, *Critical Thinking in the Classroom*, and *Fifty Strategies to Boost Cognitive Engagement*.

She earned a bachelor's degree from Georgetown College, a master's degree from the University of Kentucky, and a doctorate in K–12 education leadership from the University of Louisville.

To book Rebecca Stobaugh for professional development, contact pd@SolutionTree.com.

# Introduction

Do you remember your first year of teaching? I do, and I was terrible. I was energetic and I worked hard, but my underdeveloped speaking skills, fact-oriented teaching style, and weak approach to classroom management left my students chronically disengaged. How could I redesign my classroom to create stronger student engagement? I knew I could do better, and my students deserved more.

As a first step, I sought to make students do the work during class sessions instead of defaulting to leading class most of the time. Instead of lecturing on a topic, I tried different methods of allowing students to thoughtfully engage in the lesson. Shifting to a model where the student was the worker meant that I planned tasks where all students participated in small-group discussions centered around critical thinking tasks. For example, I posted a quote from a public figure and asked students to determine how the quote connected to what we were learning in class. Students stood up, formed two lines, and shared their thoughts with a partner. After a few minutes of conversation, students in one line took three steps to the right and formed new pairs. This activity allowed students to compare their thinking with peers and refine their ideas. My students were on their way to taking ownership of their learning. I often now say, "Whoever is the worker is the learner."

Next, I focused on shifting my instructional style. The fact-based topical structure I was relying on made me feel like I was teaching on autopilot, asking students to quickly pump out memorized information. I wasn't seeing the kind of cognitive engagement I knew my students were capable of; they weren't engaged in deep learning that would stick with them long term, and they were failing summative assessments. This approach was not working! I knew I had to merge student engagement with cognitively demanding tasks for students to meet instructional goals. Every time I looked at Bloom's taxonomy revised (Anderson & Krathwohl, 2001), I recognized that my instructional strategies weren't supporting my students to move above the lower levels of *remember*, *understand*, and *apply*. Fortunately, I was able to acquire curriculum materials that embedded *analyze* and *evaluate* tasks requiring deep cognitive processing. Utilizing these materials helped me understand how to design my own activities and assessments that were cognitively demanding and ensured long-term retention.

By my second year in the classroom, I noticed student engagement was steadily improving, and I was more satisfied with the classroom culture we were creating. But there was still something missing. With a background in middle and high school education, I was accustomed to seeing students sitting in desks for long periods of time. But when I integrated movement tasks, the students were more focused and positive. That caught my attention. I began to research other strategies for active learning and incorporating movement tasks. Movement integration proved to be the missing piece I needed to maximize student engagement in my classroom.

# Two Factors to Improve Student Engagement

My experience in boosting student engagement led me to write this book. In the following chapters, I aim to help teachers find their unique paths to improving student engagement through two factors: (1) cognitive engagement and (2) movement integration.

Let's start with cognitive engagement—every teacher has seen their fair share of disengaged students. While teachers have little control over the *outside* factors that influence students, they can create an environment *inside* the classroom that inspires students to engage in meaningful learning. So, what is cognitive engagement? In *Fifty Strategies to Boost Cognitive Engagement*, I note Douglas Fisher, Nancy Frey, Russell Quaglia, Dominique Smith, and Lisa Lande's (2018) description of *cognitive engagement* as the psychological investment a student brings to their learning:

> When students are cognitively engaged, they might lose track of time and say things like, "Is class already over?" Some other attributes of cognitive engagement include persevering and learning from experiences, sharing learning with others, and enthusiastically engaging in the learning process. (p. 7)

If we as teachers want students to respond differently to their learning, we have to offer learning that looks different from the status quo. How does this different way of learning look? Teachers limit the amount of time they talk and instead incorporate student discussions to maximize engagement. When previously several students would participate by answering teacher-directed questions, now many students engage in discussing topics and questions. These student-centered groups provide opportunities for greater student engagement and the sharing of different ideas and perspectives. Research reveals the brain prefers novelty and ignores situations that seem unimportant or routine, or what students might say seem *boring*. When fewer portions of the brain are stimulated, there is less engagement, which leads to lower learning outcomes. Dr. Judy Willis (TED, 2013), a neurologist who became a teacher, explains that when the brain is unstimulated, higher-thinking processing is shut off, which allows more reactive responses to lead the way. When this happens, students' brains struggle to focus on instruction and instead divert to identifying threatening situations or creating their own stimulation, typically in the form of negative, off-task behaviors. Disengaged students are often not learning and can be a challenge to manage. However, if teachers consider new ways to design lessons, instruction can be motivating and interesting for students.

The second factor in keeping students engaged is integrating movement. You might have noticed that students are more likely to buy in to their learning when it involves movement. Have you ever wondered why that is? A traditional approach to education treats the mind and body as separate and distinct systems—our five senses relay information to the brain, and we think about how to act on that information—a philosophy known as *mind-body dualism* (Britannica, n.d.). Think about a typical day at school: students' time in the classroom revolves around learning activities that primarily engage the intellect, while movement of the body is relegated to recess, physical education class, or periodic brain breaks. However, advances in neuroscience challenge this dualistic mind-body split.

*Embodied cognition*, a growing branch within the field of cognitive science that theorizes that the body and mind are not separate but interconnected, demonstrates that cognitive processes are intertwined with the senses and motor functions. Cognitive scientist Guy Claxton (as cited in Meserve, 2015) explains:

> The body, the gut, the senses, the immune system, the lymphatic system, are so instantaneously and so complicatedly interacting with the brain that you can't draw a line across the neck and say "above the line it's smart and below the line it's menial."

Put another way, the intellect and the body's sensorimotor systems are an integrated, cohesive whole. Associate professor Manuela Macedonia (2019) describes how simply holding an apple in your hand (not thinking, writing, or talking about it) cues neurons in visual and tactile areas of the brain to connect to networks involving shape, color, and texture so that interconnected networks map all experiences related to the fruit:

> Thinking of an apple by activating the visual image, that is the shape of the fruit, will trigger other network components including the motor programs involved in grasping,

lifting, peeling . . . and chewing the fruit. . . . In fact, if we observe how children acquire language, they perform a multitude of sensorimotor acts. Children hear and repeat sequences of sounds (words), that is symbols, but these symbols are related to objects they perceive with their senses or to actions they perform. Children cannot be prevented from touching, dropping, smelling the objects and putting them in their mouths (Adams, 2016). Therefore in the brain's language, a word must be represented as a sensorimotor network that mirrors all experiences collected to the concept (Pulvermüller, 1999).

Imagine the implications for the K–12 classroom! The traditional model of education merely engages students from the neck up. What would happen if we as teachers shifted educational practice to align with what embodied cognition is telling us? What positive outcomes might result when teachers integrate movement into the classroom? I've seen it firsthand: students become more engaged in their education when teachers treat learning as a full-body experience.

# Benefits of Engagement

When teachers invest in student engagement, the whole class benefits. When students are more involved in their learning because of cognitive engagement and embodied learning, they access the additional benefits of employability and cultural responsiveness.

Creating an engaging classroom environment increases students' employability skills, those essential competencies workers need to thrive in the global workplace (McBride & Duncan-Davis, 2021). Preparing students to enter the workforce with skills suited to the demands of the 21st century is a major focus of teachers, administrators, and advocacy groups across the globe. Renée McAlpin (2017), director of EduQuality at Opportunity EduFinance, explains, "This means moving beyond teaching traditional subject areas, such as numeracy and literacy, to including a broad range of skills, such as problem solving, critical thinking, and collaboration."

What exactly are 21st century skills? They are twelve skills, grouped into three categories (Stauffer, 2022).

- Learning skills (the four Cs)
  - **Critical thinking:** Analyzing and evaluating information
  - **Creativity:** Producing something unique
  - **Collaboration:** Working with others to complete a task
  - **Communication:** Sharing ideas and solutions
- Literacy skills (IMT)
  - **Information literacy:** Comprehending facts, figures, and data
  - **Media literacy:** Knowing how to publish information online
  - **Technology literacy:** Awareness of the digital tools available
- Life skills (FLIPS)
  - **Flexibility:** Adjusting plans to meet goals
  - **Leadership:** Organizing groups to meet objectives
  - **Initiative:** Initiating tasks independently
  - **Productivity:** Focusing on efficiently completing tasks
  - **Social skills:** Effectively using verbal and nonverbal skills during interactions

Possessing these 21st century skills enables students to adjust to the changing employee landscape by learning, innovating, considering different viewpoints, communicating complex ideas, utilizing technology to create and solve problems, and resolving workplace challenges.

Most teachers know that students become more invested in mastering content when teachers create pathways for them to participate in co-creating their learning. Professor of education Geneva Gay (2010) confirms this, advocating for teachers to embrace culturally relevant teaching by "using the cultural knowledge, prior experiences, frames of reference, and performance styles of ethnically diverse students to make learning encounters more relevant to and effective for them. It teaches *to and through* the strengths of these students" (p. 31). Many teachers agree that making course content relevant to students has a large impact on student engagement (Aguilar, Ahrens, Janowicz, Sheldon,

Turner, & Willia, 2021). As teachers create a culture of engagement in the classroom, they also create opportunities for culturally relevant instruction. This means designing instructional experiences with students' ages, strengths, interests, and diverse cultural expressions in mind. When this happens, students notice, and they feel safe, seen, appreciated, and celebrated. They also receive a model for how to treat one another with curiosity, openness, and respect.

## This Book's Purpose and Structure

This book is about boosting student engagement through movement. It argues that students become deeply engaged in their learning when teachers create high-level instructional practices that integrate movement. In addition to providing foundational knowledge about engagement and the benefits of movement, the following chapters offer more than thirty strategies to infuse movement into your classroom and ensure high levels of student engagement. Each strategy includes a description to establish the rationale, strategy steps to guide implementation, variations to inspire alternatives, additional content area examples, and options for differentiation to illustrate how to meet diverse student needs. These sections will ensure you have numerous ideas for how to transfer these strategies directly into your classroom.

These active learning strategies are classified into three categories: (1) partners, (2) teams, and (3) games. Partner strategies include movement and high levels of student participation while engaging in rigorous tasks with partners. Team strategies include kinesthetic learning while engaging with a larger group to gain insight into various perspectives. Games strategies showcase methods to incorporate movement while increasing students' interest with a low level of competition.

The strategies profiled in this book are for all grade levels and content areas. Each strategy includes specific applications for English, mathematics, science, social studies, and humanities, or career and vocational studies. In addition, since there is a wide range of student abilities and needs in the classroom, each strategy highlights several techniques for differentiation. As with any strategy, with varied abilities and grade levels, you will want to make adjustments based on your students' unique needs. To support you in implementing these strategies, each chapter ends with discussion questions for you to consider and action steps for you to take.

Chapter 1 lays a foundation for understanding student engagement. I discuss what engagement and disengagement look like, why they happen, and why they matter in the classroom. I also take a closer look at cognitive engagement, as it is central to the strategies offered throughout the book.

Chapter 2 examines historical changes in movement patterns and how they affect students in the classroom. I share the benefits of movement integration and cover four types of movement teachers can integrate into the classroom. Finally, I share six key motivating factors that illustrate why integrating movement boosts cognitive engagement.

Chapter 3 explores how to use peer discussion to boost engagement. I start by covering the benefits students access when they work in pairs. Next, I outline how to establish context, select partners, and pose questions in advance to prepare yourself and your students to begin working with a partner. The rest of the chapter provides eleven strategies you can use to integrate movement into your classroom via peer discussions.

Chapter 4 discusses how students benefit from working in groups of three to five members. I share suggestions for assigning group members and ensuring that all students have an equal chance to participate. Finally, I offer thirteen strategies for integrating movement through group activities.

Chapter 5 demonstrates the benefits of using games in the classroom to boost student engagement. I offer steps for preparing to incorporate games and introduce twelve active learning strategies that incorporate games.

The final chapter outlines key ideas for implementing these strategies in sustainable ways that foster a culture of movement among students including classroom design, classroom climate, and classroom management.

Are you ready to evaluate your own practices and identify ways to increase student engagement, high-level thinking, and movement integration? If so, let's begin!

# CHAPTER 1

# Understanding Student Engagement

*As Mr. Dominic's social studies class of twenty-five students begins, he shows three photos of families in Iraq, Kuwait, and Syria standing outside their homes with everything they own. Mr. Dominic forms students into small groups and tasks them with analyzing the geography and hypothesizing how that geography might impact these families' daily lives. After groups share their thinking, Mr. Dominic explains that this region was where ancient Mesopotamia emerged.*

*Mr. Dominic assigns students to read a passage about the geography of ancient Mesopotamia, noting how geography impacted early settlements. As students read the article, they complete a graphic organizer divided into two columns: Knew and New. Students record information from the article they had already learned in the Knew column and then record any new learning in the New column. As students finish reading, Mr. Dominic instructs them to stand up with their graphic organizer, find one partner to discuss and compare their answers with, and develop two open-ended questions about how geography impacted ancient settlement in Mesopotamia. Mr. Dominic uses the student-generated questions to drive subsequent classroom discussion.*

Would you characterize Mr. Dominic's classroom as one with high student engagement? Why or why not? What factors come to mind when you think about what an engaging classroom looks and feels like? Use the questionnaire in figure 1.1 to check your understanding of student engagement.

| Student Engagement Questionnaire |
| --- |
| **For each question, check the box that best applies to you.** |
| How would you rate your understanding of the concept of student engagement? |
| ❏ Have not explored the concept of student engagement |
| ❏ Partially understand the basic ideas of student engagement |
| ❏ Understand the basic ideas of student engagement |
| ❏ Completely understand multiple ways to engage students |
| How would you rate your understanding of the concept of cognitive engagement? |
| ❏ Have not explored the concept of cognitive engagement |
| ❏ Partially understand the basic ideas of cognitive engagement |
| ❏ Understand the basic ideas of cognitive engagement |
| ❏ Completely understand multiple ways to cognitively engage students |
| How would you rate your understanding of the concept of movement integration? |
| ❏ Have not explored the concept of movement integration |
| ❏ Partially understand the basic ideas of movement integration |
| ❏ Understand the basic ideas of movement integration |
| ❏ Completely understand multiple ways to use movement integration |

**Figure 1.1:** Rate your understanding.

In this chapter, I help you develop a foundational understanding of what student engagement is all about. I discuss what disengagement looks like, why it happens, and why it's a problem. Then I explore what it looks like for students to be engaged, how to create engagement, and how it benefits students. Finally, I home in on a specific type of engagement—cognitive engagement, which I discussed in the introduction (page 2). You'll have a chance to reflect using discussion questions and action steps before moving on to chapter 2.

## Disengagement

What does disengagement look like in the classroom? Why is it a problem? And what can teachers do to avoid it? These are a few of the questions we'll address throughout this section.

Data from secondary students reveal many are disengaged, with disengagement increasing through middle school and into high school (Whole Child Symposium, 2016). Senior consultant at Gallup Tim Hodges (2018) reports that fewer than half of student respondents stated they were engaged in school (47 percent), with around one-fourth reporting they were "not engaged" (29 percent), and the remainder stating they were "actively disengaged" (24 percent). See figure 1.2 for a graphic representation of the data.

Hodges (2018) also notes that fifth graders reported higher levels of engagement, at 74 percent. However, these levels depict a negative trajectory from fifth grade through high school. Roughly half of middle school students claim high levels of engagement whereas only about one-third of high school students claim high levels of engagement (Hodges, 2018).

Disengagement is a problem. Chronically disengaged students are at risk for academic failure, behavioral problems, social seclusion, and other poor outcomes (Gupta & Reeves, 2021). Every teacher can recall students whose disengagement resulted in poor school attendance, frequent disciplinary referrals, or failing social connections. What leads students to become disengaged?

Students become disengaged for various reasons. A common cause lies with instruction: low-level tasks fail to engage the brain and stimulate thought (Boser & Rosenthal, 2012). Sometimes over-scaffolding instruction by adding significant supports like coaching and modeling removes the intellectual curiosity needed to ignite learning. Critiquing the trend of trying to make up ground through high-dose tutoring and pull-out programs focused on remediation, author and teacher educator Zaretta Hammond states, "We make up ground by actually using intellectual curiosity to turbocharge students' engagement. We need to *water up* the curriculum and instruction, not water it down" (as cited in Rebora, 2021).

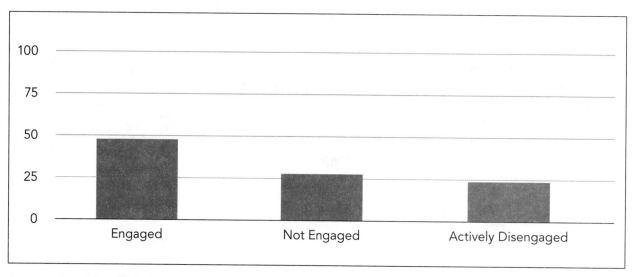

*Source: Adapted from Hodges, 2018*

**Figure 1.2:** Student engagement levels.

Disengagement is also caused by the amount of time teachers talk in the classroom. A teacher who does most of the work may be doing this unconsciously, simply replicating the teaching style they experienced in their K–12 education. However, current research demonstrates that this style of teaching does not maximize student learning and often results in losing students' attention, asking discouraging questions, and presenting information too quickly (Wilson & Korn, 2007).

While some students and teachers excel in a predominately verbal classroom, many do not. Listening to lectures places the students in a passive learning role, whereas collaborating with peers to participate in the learning allows students to take an active role. For example, researchers Jennifer Knight and William Wood (2005) find that interactive classes generate significantly higher learning gains and better conceptual understanding.

Disengagement can also result when students' interests, identities, and cultural frameworks differ from those of their teachers. Teachers sometimes connect content with examples that relate to their background but fail to relate to students' real-world experiences. I saw this happen as I observed a new teacher leading an economics lesson. The teacher demonstrated a concept by giving an example in which students paid for their lunch. The students stared quizzically at the teacher. Finally, one student raised a hand and informed the teacher that none of the students paid for lunch in their school. The teacher, from a middle-class background, was operating from a different socioeconomic framework than the students, who were from predominately low-income communities. Gay (2010) refers to this as *cultural blindness*, arguing that "teaching is most effective when ecological factors, such as prior experiences, community settings, cultural backgrounds, and ethnic identities of teachers and students, are included" in classroom instruction (p. 22).

Pause for a moment and reflect on what you've read so far. What does disengagement look like in your classroom? Do you recognize any of the preceding causes of disengagement negatively impacting your students? Use the checklist in figure 1.3 to note behaviors you have observed.

| Checking for Disengagement in the Classroom |
| --- |
| **Place a check mark beside the behaviors students exhibit in the classroom.** |
| ❑ Texting |
| ❑ Playing games on a device |
| ❑ Sleeping |
| ❑ Disrupting the flow of learning |
| ❑ Remaining silent during class discussions |
| ❑ Completing tasks with minimal effort |

**Figure 1.3:** Checking for disengagement in the classroom.

What other signs of disengagement would you add to the checklist? Which of your students are disengaged and when? It can be discouraging to face disengagement among your students, but the good news is there are effective methods to address it. When you know how to recognize disengagement and understand why it's happening, you can work to change it without forcing yourself into uncomfortable and unproductive confrontations with students. Next, let's examine what student engagement looks like and how it's created.

# Engagement

Student engagement can be defined as "the level of meaningful student involvement in the learning process often displayed through concentrated attention and focus on learning tasks" (Howard, Bingener, & Howard, 2021). When students are engaged, they complete tasks because they really want to do them and see the value of them, rather than because they're compelled to complete them through extrinsic rewards or desires to comply.

Engagement is related to novelty and variety. Routine tasks cause boredom, whereas fun and unique tasks are more likely to spark engagement. However, *lessons should not just be fun for the sake of fun*; their purpose is to create novel learning. Entertaining tasks may briefly energize learners but will not sustain engagement for long-term learning, whereas tasks that spur student curiosity and cognitive engagement increase students' academic achievement (Hassinger-Das & Hirsh-Pasek, 2018). For example, consider a class is learning about westward expansion in North America. One teacher assigns students to follow a list of instructions to make a model of a wagon settlers used to move west.

Another teacher assigns students to work in groups and use their knowledge of available resources to construct a plan for leading a group of settlers west. The first group of students is tasked with learning the information by passively following instructions, whereas the second group of students is tasked with thinking creatively and collaboratively to solve a problem. Which group do you think has a stronger chance for long-term learning about the challenges of westward migration?

Engagement is also connected to student interests. Phillip Schlechty (2011) contends that teachers should design classroom tasks to be more interesting, even if the content studied is uninteresting. Teachers can design tasks aligned to content standards in a way that makes students want to participate and engage. This is where cultural responsiveness comes in. Hammond asserts that culturally responsive teaching empowers teachers to make "'cognitive hooks' between the learner's context, interests, cultural knowledge, and the new content in the curriculum" (as cited in Rebora, 2021).

I witnessed firsthand the effectiveness of culturally responsive teaching during my time as a principal in a rural area where student state assessment mathematics scores were low. After observing the mathematics teachers, I realized they were passionate about teaching their subject and serving the students, but the assessments were not as rigorous as the state assessment, which included word problems. The mathematics teachers decided to address this challenge by including a daily word problem related to students' interests. During walkthroughs, I observed students answering mathematics problems about measuring acceleration of race cars, calculating the distance between a hunter and an animal, and determining the best deal on a cell phone. Students not only applied their mathematics in cognitively complex problems, but they also recognized how mathematics can help them in everyday life. When the teachers connected to students' interests, mathematics scores soared.

Take a moment to reflect on your experiences with student engagement. When you think about your classes, what percentage of your students would you describe as engaged? What percentage would you describe as disengaged? Read the descriptors in figure 1.4 and insert a percentage in the first column for each item.

What factors would you cite that contribute to those percentages? There are many external factors influencing students' investment in learning that are outside a teacher's control. To boost engagement, teachers must consider the factors they can influence inside the classroom. What adjustments can you make to center your class around high-engagement behaviors? Read each statement in figure 1.5 and indicate in the first column whether it's true (T) or false (F).

How many of the statements in figure 1.5 describe your teaching beliefs and actions? While teachers can't affect external factors that influence student engagement, they can create an engaging classroom environment. Teachers must acknowledge that they have a strong impact on ensuring student engagement and then be willing to adopt new instructional practices to boost classroom engagement.

| Percent | High-Engagement Behaviors |
|---------|---------------------------|
|  | Remain focused on content tasks |
|  | Persist with content tasks despite difficulties |
|  | Maximize effort, time, and attention to commit to work |
| **Percent** | **Low-Engagement Behaviors** |
|  | Remain attentive only when extrinsic awards are given |
|  | Devote minimal time, energy, and effort to a task |
|  | Become distracted easily or frequently distract others |

Source: Adapted from Schlechty, 2011.

**Figure 1.4:** Gauging student engagement.

| True or False | Engagement Patterns |
|---|---|
| | When designing classroom tasks, I thoughtfully consider the ways my students like to learn and I ensure their interests are represented in instructional strategies. |
| | When students are less engaged than I expect, I analyze my teaching strategies and assignments to identify ways to change this pattern. |
| | I believe that my teaching strategies and assignments largely impact the level of my students' engagement. |
| | To increase student engagement in my class, I encourage colleagues to recommend other methods that can bolster student engagement levels. |

Source: Adapted from Schlechty, 2011.

**Figure 1.5:** Analyzing engagement patterns.

# Dimensions of Engagement

Now that we've established a general understanding of student engagement in the classroom, let's look more specifically at various aspects of engagement. Researchers James Appleton, Sandra Christenson, and Michael Furlong (2008) assert there are three dimensions to engagement.

1. **Behavioral:** Observable engagement indicators include completing assignments, participating in class discussions, and following classroom rules. Students are on task and immersed in academic work.

2. **Affective:** Emotional engagement refers to students' feelings about the learning process including their interest and curiosity. Students have positive feelings toward learning, school, and friends.

3. **Cognitive:** Psychological effort students wield during the learning process as they construct new understandings. Students are invested in co-creating their learning.

Teachers observe the behavioral and affective dimensions in students' physical and nonverbal actions. They can measure them using observation or student surveys. But teachers must gauge cognitive engagement through the academic work students produce. One study contends that a student is first emotionally engaged (affective) through positive relationships with peers and teachers. Then, behavioral engagement emerges as the student actively participates and perseveres through challenges (Sumbera, 2017).

*Cognitive engagement* is defined as the extent to which students willingly invest their effort in academic tasks. In addition, cognitive engagement is connected to levels of thinking. Teachers can focus on this dimension of engagement as they develop instructional plans that are cognitively demanding.

Authors Pérsida Himmele and William Himmele (2011) illustrate the interaction between the cognitive and behavioral dimensions of engagement through four quadrants. (Visit https://bit.ly/3Q103bT to see a visual representation of the four quadrants.) Cognitive engagement (*cognition*) and behavioral engagement (*participation*) are measured as either high or low.

1. **Low cognition and low participation:** Students are passive learners, and the learning is very low level with no deep processing to promote enduring understanding. Instruction is teacher-led with few students participating.

2. **Low cognition and high participation:** Students may find classroom tasks fun and interesting, but they still don't engage in the critical thinking that would ensure long-term learning. Hammond states, "Too often we reduce engagement to hands-on 'activities' or to a lesson that's fun and interactive, but we don't necessarily connect that interactivity to academic rigor or cognitive capacity building" (as cited in Rebora, 2021).

3. **High cognition and low participation:** Cognitively demanding experiences cue students to think critically, reflect, and solve problems, but only a few students might engage in the experience.

4.  **High cognition and high participation:** Students are fully immersed in a rigorous learning process with all students analyzing, evaluating, and creating. Students engage in active learning that "stimulates thought, expands ideas, and gives students the ability to solve complex problems, comprehend what they learn, and synthesize new information into existing schema" (Howard, Bingener, & Howard, 2021).

High participation describes students who are interested and actively involved in the learning process. High-cognition experiences are those that are relevant and ignite intellectual curiosity and meaning making. Provocative questions, experiments, and inquiry ignite students' curiosity to maximize engagement. Optimally, by designing instruction that meets the criteria of high cognition and high participation, teachers create equity and encourage all students to strive to meet their intellectual capacity (Rebora, 2021).

The goal of this book is to detail specific ways to maximize cognition and participation with rigorous instruction and student participation. Table 1.1 illustrates examples at each level of cognitive engagement.

This framework illustrates that engagement and cognitive demand are often dictated by how teachers design instruction. Not all classroom tasks are the same. Different types of assignments produce different levels of learning. Let's consider an example to illustrate this point.

Ms. May wants to integrate student use of technology into her social studies lesson. She assigns students in groups to create a digital presentation about one of the U.S. founding fathers. Students search online for information and paste it into their presentations. Notice that this approach fails to achieve high participation and high cognition. Which quadrant would you place this activity in?

**Table 1.1** Examples of Engagement Quadrants

| High Cognition and Low Participation | High Cognition and High Participation |
|---|---|
| Consider the following examples of high cognition and low participation. | Consider the following examples of high cognition and high participation. |
| • A teacher poses critical-thinking questions to a few students.<br>• After watching a video, several students share their ideas aloud with the class, explaining the reasons for an explosion based on scientific principles they have studied.<br>• A teacher asks the class to evaluate whether the character in a book they're reading made a good choice. The teacher selects a few students to share their thinking and evidence from the story to support their viewpoint. | • Students critique peers' work based on a rubric.<br>• Students examine a piece of writing and highlight evidence to support each claim. Students form pairs and evaluate if each claim was adequately defended.<br>• After reviewing historical evidence, students decide to approve or disapprove of a historical leader's actions. Each group creates a list of historical evidence to support their stance to be shared in a classroom debate. |
| **Low Cognition and Low Participation** | **Low Cognition and High Participation** |
| Consider the following examples of low cognition and low participation. | Consider the following examples of low cognition and high participation. |
| • A teacher conducts a lecture.<br>• A teacher reads to the class.<br>• A teacher asks students to state their favorite character from a novel they're reading. A few students share answers aloud with the class but do not provide a rationale. | • Students play a memorization game matching cards to definitions.<br>• Students review vocabulary with all students participating in an online game.<br>• In pairs, students play a multiplication tables game, trying to correctly answer multiplication problems and arranging correctly answered cards in a stack. |

Now imagine that Ms. May restructures the assignment for higher-level learning to create less opportunity for students to copy information directly from the internet. She presents the following four assignment options and invites students to work with a partner on one of the tasks.

1. Select a founding father you think would be an effective leader in our government if he were alive today. Prepare a digital presentation to defend your reasoning.

2. Select a founding father who is similar to you in several ways. Explain the similarities in a written essay citing historical evidence.

3. Select a founding father you believe most impacted the U.S. government. Prepare an argumentative case for an upcoming classroom debate.

4. Select a founding father that could also be considered a traitor. Create a website with historical evidence to argue your case.

Notice in each of these assignments all students would have to be engaged to create a final product. There are different product options and prompts intended to spur diverse student interest. Each of these tasks is cognitively demanding, requiring students to think at a high level. Which quadrant would you place this activity in?

When teachers design effective tasks, students can be engaged and challenged. Teachers can positively impact cognitive engagement through their development of effective instructional plans. As teachers incorporate creative and critical thinking tasks in tandem with interesting and compelling activities, students become engaged and take ownership of their learning.

## Discussion Questions

As you reflect on this chapter, consider the following five questions.

1. How would you define engagement?

2. How would you define cognitive engagement?

3. How would your students benefit from high-cognition and high-participation instructional activities?

4. What two causes of disengagement can you identify in your classroom?

5. What research presented in this chapter is most compelling to you?

## Action Steps

Use the following three activities to put this chapter's concepts to work in your own classroom.

1. Take an idea presented in the chapter and use or adapt it for your classroom.

2. Have a colleague observe your classroom and classify it according to the cognitive engagement quadrants (Himmele & Himmele, 2011).

3. Make a list of student behaviors in your classroom and classify them as *engaged* or *disengaged*. Place it where you'll be cued to revisit it as you progress through this book so you can monitor your classroom for signs of increased student engagement.

# CHAPTER 2

# Integrating Movement Into the Classroom

*Drew was a popular and good-natured student and a football player. He participated in class and did not misbehave often. I did notice an unusual pattern in his behavior, though. Although it wasn't disruptive, Drew had a habit of getting up several times during class to sharpen his pencil. As he returned to his seat, he regained his concentration and began working.*

It's only in hindsight that I understand Drew's behavior: I think the repetitive motion was his way of *sharpening* his focus on classroom tasks. How could I design a classroom where students like Drew wouldn't need to sharpen pencils unnecessarily but could instead learn while moving?

In chapter 1 (page 5), we explored the role of cognitive engagement in boosting overall student engagement. I started by laying the foundation of cognitive engagement before talking about movement for a reason: embedding movement into instruction is more than just letting students move their bodies for the fun of it. Movement integration is about designing instruction in a way that uses movement to *facilitate learning*. When teachers recognize students as whole people—understanding that the body and brain are not separate but interconnected and intricately involved in the learning process—they are able to design instruction that engages each student individually and the classroom as a collective.

In this chapter, I discuss how historical changes in movement habits negatively impact students and how the benefits of movement integration can counter these effects. I outline four main types of movement integration: (1) focus-based, (2) brain-centered, (3) games-based, and (4) content-oriented. Finally, I reinforce that movement integration is a powerful tool for boosting cognitive engagement. The chapter ends with discussion questions and action steps.

## Historical Changes in Movement

Societal and educational changes have led to decreased movement over time in North America (Woessner, Tacey, Levinger-Limor, Parker, Levinger, & Levinger, 2021) and worldwide (López-Bueno, López-Sánchez, Casajús, Calatayud, Tully, & Smith, 2021). Schools have reduced students' time spent in physical education classes during school hours, and electronic gaming has replaced many physical activities for students after school. Unfortunately, this is counterproductive. As developmental molecular biologist John Medina (2008) writes, "Cutting off physical exercise—the very activity most likely to promote cognitive performance—to do better on a test score is like trying to gain weight by starving yourself" (p. 25).

The largest amount of uninterrupted sedentary time for students occurs during the school day, as classroom culture requires them to be seated and silent for long stretches. Research indicates that middle school students spend up to 70 percent of the school day sitting (Carson et al., 2013). This sedentary environment is concerning, connected with early adolescent students' lower ability to maintain attention and remain on task

(Van der Niet, Smith, Scherder, Oosterlaan, Hartman, & Visscher, 2014).

Fortunately, research suggests that kinesthetic learning strategies boost academic performance. In the 1930s, researchers began to explore the connection between cognition and physical activity, finding associations in the brain between movement and thinking (Hillman, Erickson, & Kramer, 2008). The section of the brain that processes movement also processes learning (Middleton & Strick, 1994).

The following researchers also find that boosting oxygen through movement improves brain functioning.

- When students move, they get more oxygen to the brain, which increases energy, lowers stress, and enables them to be prepared for learning (Merriam & Bierema, 2013).

- Physical movement can have a positive impact on cognition by increasing blood flow to the brain, infusing it with more oxygen and glucose, thus improving the brain's function (Hall, 2007).

- Simply standing can increase the heart rate and blood flow by around five to eight percent in a few seconds (Krock & Hartung, 1992).

The takeaway for teachers? Movement increases cognitive functioning, which supports students' long-term learning. When students learn through movement, they create new and stronger neural connections to enhance memory.

# Benefits of Movement Integration

As I mentioned in the introduction (page 1), this book is built on embodied cognition, the field of study that investigates the mind and body not as separate entities but as an integrated system. In the following sections, we'll explore four main benefits of integrating movement into the classroom: (1) positive health outcomes, (2) collaborative culture, (3) academic achievement, and (4) classroom management. While most teachers agree that maximizing student thinking is important, some teachers view movement as more appropriate for elementary school students. However, the positive attributes for integrating movement extend to all levels of learners.

## Positive Health Outcomes

Many industries integrate movement into the workplace to increase engagement, improve health, and boost productivity. The corporate world uses walking meetings to promote a healthy lifestyle and combine thinking and walking (Clayton, Thomas, & Smothers, 2015). North Carolina's Eat Smart, Move More movement guides professionals to make movement part of meetings, conferences, and events, and includes ideas such as organizing a group walk, providing a free pass to a local recreation center, and including movement breaks in the agenda (North Carolina Department of Health and Human Services, n.d.). Toni Yancey, in her TEDx Talk, "What's Good for the Waistline is Good for the Bottom Line" (TED, 2012), asserts that even small amounts of movement for adults and students can increase focus, engagement, self-efficacy, energy levels, cognitive processing, and morale. Physical exercise is connected to positive health outcomes, including emotional well-being, improved sleep, and completing daily tasks more easily (2018 Physical Activity Guidelines Advisory Committee, 2018).

Research suggests that incorporating physical activity into instruction promotes healthy outcomes for students too. In a study of elementary mathematics classes, researchers followed students who integrated movement into their learning, which they measured with pedometers and accelerometers. In the active classes, students engaged in physical activities such as moving during a game to indicate true or false statements and organizing into groups to illustrate fractions. Conversely, students in the inactive classrooms followed the traditional curriculum. Students in the physically active mathematics classes were significantly more active throughout the day than those in the nonintervention group (Erwin, Abel, Beighle, & Beets, 2011).

Studies also illustrate that students incur negative health outcomes when classes are sedentary. For example, a 2016 study finds that students who sit in the classroom for long periods report worse physical profiles across a range of cardio-metabolic markers (Carson et al., 2016). Numerous other studies have confirmed that physically active classroom lessons can positively impact children's physical activity levels (Norris, Shelton, Dunsmuir, Duke-Williams, & Stamatakis, 2015; Owen, Parker, Van

Zenden, MacMillan, Astell-Burt, & Lonsdale, 2016; Watson, Timperio, Brown, Best, & Hesketh, 2017).

## Collaborative Culture

Allowing students to learn through movement opens the door to a collaborative classroom culture. Increased student movement can lead to heightened interest and excitement about the learning (Mavilidi, Okely, Chandler, & Paas, 2016; Vazou & Skrade, 2017). Teachers know intuitively what the research suggests: students are more lively, excited, and invested in classroom learning when they actively work together rather than sit in silence completing individual work. Professors Suzanne Lindt and Stacia Miller (2017) also find that students are significantly more enthusiastic, engaged, and focused when lessons incorporate movement.

In addition, using pairs, teams, and games that invite all students to participate and co-create the learning cultivates a dynamic and supportive environment. Hammond (as cited in Rebora, 2021) suggests that when teachers create environments that ignite students' inherent curiosity, teachers boost engagement and equity:

> When we think about equity as making sure every student reaches their intellectual capacity so they *can* carry a heavier cognitive load—so that they can take part in deep learning that is rigorous, for example—then we see how critical it is to create the kind of intellectual curiosity and engagement that allows us to kick-start students' information processing and meaning making. . . . For me, the question is: *Do we do enough to create classroom environments for students to be intellectually curious?* The problem is not typically with the kids, who always come in with intellectual curiosity on some level. It's with the environments we are creating.

In addition to supporting students' curiosity, opportunities for movement validate alternative styles of learning, affirm various skills and interests as assets, and celebrate diverse cultures. Gay (2002) explains:

> Cooperative group learning arrangements and peer coaching fit well with the communal cultural systems of African, Asian, Native, and Latino American groups (Gay, 2000; Spring, 1995). . . . Motion and movement, music,

> frequent variability in tasks and formats, novelty, and dramatic elements in teaching improve [academic performance] . . . culturally relevant examples have positive effects on the academic achievement of ethnically diverse students. (pp. 112–113)

A movement-rich classroom environment where students frequently collaborate, bring their strengths to the group, and engage in ways that are authentic to their home culture maximizes student engagement.

## Academic Achievement

With the positive benefits of movement for boosting learning, including enhancing learner motivation and morale, it is not surprising the data support that kinesthetic learning experiences can lead to positive academic outcomes. When students move, the body helps the brain to think, create, and perform at a higher level (Holt, Bartee, & Heelan, 2013).

Consider the following findings:

- Researcher Annie Murphy Paul (2021) finds that students engaged in movement while learning retain 76 percent of the content as compared to those who memorize information without moving and retain only 37 percent of the material. Even with low cognitive tasks, student movement can improve academic success.

- When teachers utilize classroom-based physical activity, students increase their content knowledge, skills, and test scores in core subjects such as mathematics and reading fluency (Adams-Blair & Oliver, 2011; Browning, Edson, Kimani, & Aslan-Tutak, 2014; Erwin, Fedewa, & Ahn, 2012). Movement often positively affects student interest, leading to high participation and cognition.

- Research studies in second through fifth grades reveal significant improvements in mathematics learning, fluency, and classroom engagement when integrating student movement (Szabo-Reed, Willis, Lee, Hillman, Washburn, & Donnelly, 2019; Vazou & Skrade, 2017). While some students might lack interest in mathematics, when teachers effectively integrate movement into learning mathematical principles, achievement increases.

- A 2018 study finds that school students who walked for ten minutes had significantly higher scores on mathematical problem-solving tasks, as compared with students who did not walk (Mualem et al., 2018).

In addition to increasing academic performance, physical activity interventions enhance executive-function skills including working memory, flexible thinking, and self-control in children (Egger, Conzelmann, & Schmidt, 2018; Schmidt, Jäger, Egger, Roebers, & Conzelmann, 2015). These core executive functions are foundational for students' social, physical, psychological, and emotional development. Researchers Mirko Schmidt and colleagues (2017) assert that appropriate development in these areas is positively associated with school readiness and academic achievement. While some educators consider instructional strategies that incorporate student movement as childish or a waste of time, research contradicts these beliefs. Movement has a positive impact on academic achievement for students of all ages.

### Classroom Management

Do you often lack focus after sitting and working on a task for a long period of time? I do! Students who are expected to sit still for extended periods often exhibit negative behaviors. Students who struggle to be attentive, stay focused, and concentrate on routine tasks often cope by engaging in off-task behaviors that pose classroom management challenges.

Teachers can counter these effects by incorporating movement into the classroom. Data show that movement integration positively impacts students' abilities to stay on task (Owen et al., 2016; Watson et al., 2017). In addition, active learning experiences have been shown to reduce classroom management issues (Centers for Disease Control and Prevention, 2014; Ferlazzo, 2020). Research suggests that daily recess or physical activity breaks in the classroom can lower off-task behaviors and increase appropriate behaviors (Camahalan & Ipock, 2015; Jarrett, Maxwell, Dickerson, Hoge, Davies, & Yetley, 1998). And researchers Faye Marsha Camahalan and Amanda Ipock (2015) report that physical activity breaks increase attentiveness and positive classroom behaviors.

Whether we're talking about recess or short physical breaks between instruction, these movement opportunities grant students an appropriate time and way to refocus. Not only is movement good for students, but it also enhances the classroom environment for teachers. Writing for *Education Week*, teacher Larry Ferlazzo (2020) notes, "One of the most effective (and free) ways to improve attitudes, increase retention, and improve student focus is to lead students in simple movement activities." When students have the opportunity to learn through movement, the whole class benefits.

## Types of Movement Integration

While movement integration is common in elementary schools, it is less prevalent in middle and high schools, which may account for escalating disengagement in secondary education (ASCD, 2016). There are a variety of ways to incorporate movement into the classroom, which I discuss in the following sections. Recall the opening scene in chapter 2 (page 13). For students like Drew, who need movement to stay engaged, *focus-based* movement can be helpful. *Brain-based* movement is appropriate for breaking up long instructional periods and helping students recharge. Teachers may choose *game-based* activities to boost morale and allow students to connect with their peers or blow off steam. Finally, taking movement to the next level is possible when teachers choose *content-oriented* strategies that pair academic content with movement, increasing cognitive engagement.

### Focus-Based

Fidgeting behaviors—such as when students tap their fingers, shake their legs, or kick the leg of their desk—have traditionally been suppressed in the classroom. However, psychologist Carey Heller (2017) writes that professionals and parents are beginning to recognize that they can harness fidgeting to help students improve focus: "Individuals fidget when they are bored, unfocused, and understimulated. . . . Harnessing fidgeting (not stopping it) turns uncontrolled tapping, leg shaking, etc. into controlled movements. In turn, this can lead to increased focus." Consider the following ideas to offer fidgety students small ways to move to boost focus (tailored as needed to elementary and secondary student needs).

- **Manipulatives:** In a basket accessible to students during class time, stock classroom-acceptable manipulatives, such as the following.
  - Stress balls
  - Silly putty
  - Fidget spinners
  - Brain teaser puzzles

- **Energizers:** Interrupt extended periods of sitting or independent work with short activity breaks to help students refocus and boost energy, such as the following.
  - Roll a die or select a numbered card that indicates how many repetitions of a movement students will perform.
  - Write several different movements on popsicle sticks. A student can select a stick and the class will perform that movement.
  - Say to students, "If you are ready to learn, please _____." Fill in the blank with a movement (for example, *clap twice* or *stomp your feet three times*).
  - Instruct students to touch two walls and return to their seats.
  - Instruct students to stand and take a stretch break.

## Brain-Centered

Research suggests that the brain exhausts its nutrient stores, mainly glucose, after twenty minutes of rigorous thinking (Ampel, Muraven, & McNay, 2018; Hattie & Yates, 2014; Sousa, 2012). This can lead students to zone out in the middle or at the end of a lesson that stretches beyond that twenty-minute mark. To support students' brains to recharge, offer short brain breaks from instruction. Consider the following resources (by accessing the URL or QR code), adjusting them as needed for your grade level and content area.

- **Take a Break!:** This teacher toolbox from the Colorado Education Initiative (n.d.) offers a variety of activities for secondary students and includes lesson plan templates, printable activity cards, and online resources. (Visit https://bit.ly/3MYtrxU)

- **Jammin' Minute videos:** These short videos lead elementary students in quick, active exercises. (Visit https://youtu.be/IXGCRUJI7t8 for an example.)

- **The Atlas Mission:** This website offers ten easy ways to engage preschool or elementary students in classroom movement. (Visit https://bit.ly/3OJJSis)

- **GoNoodle:** GoNoodle has a wealth of fun songs and dances to get elementary students moving. (Visit www.gonoodle.com)

- **Jack Hartman:** Hartman's YouTube channel has a variety of playlists for brain breaks that reinforce elementary content. (Visit www.youtube.com/c/JackHartmann/channels)

- **Dancing Classrooms:** Dancing Classrooms is a program devoted to promoting social dance at school. (Visit https://dancingclassrooms.org)

- **Dr. Jean:** Dr. Jean's website includes videos and PowerPoint slides teachers can use to facilitate brain breaks and reinforce core knowledge for elementary students. (Visit https://drjean.org/html/powerPoints.html)

- **Get Movin' Activity Breaks:** Get Movin' offers a PDF with nearly one hundred pages of brain break ideas for elementary classrooms. (Visit https://bit.ly/3A9DE86)

Any of these resources will get your students up out of their seat and keep them engaged in their learning.

Visit **go.SolutionTree.com/studentengagement** or follow the QR code for a list of live links to access these resources.

## Games-Based

Games are a great way to involve the whole class in movement during activity breaks. Some class games are solely for having fun, sharing laughs, and taking a pause from learning while other games incorporate thinking components. Consider the following options, which may be adjusted to meet students' unique needs.

- **Detective:** Appoint one student to be the *detective* and another to be the *leader*. Instruct the class to complete a motion (for example, clapping their hands). When the detective opens their eyes, the leader changes the motion. The detective tries to determine which classmate is the leader.

- **Balloon up:** Blow up a balloon and divide the class into teams. Instruct students to sit at their desks, choose a spot on the floor, or stand in place. The teams try to keep the balloon in the air, not allowing it to hit the ground. Add more balloons to increase the challenge.

- **Rock-paper-scissors:** Instruct students to pair off for a few rounds of rock-paper-scissors. To extend the game, conduct a tournament.

- **Would you rather:** On opposite sides of the classroom, designate spaces for students to occupy based on two answer choices. Call out "Would you rather . . . ?" questions and allow students to move to the side of the classroom that represents their choice.

- **High five or fist bump:** Instruct students to high five or fist bump as many classmates as possible in two minutes.

- **Statues:** Instruct students to spread out across the classroom. Play music and allow students to dance, move around the classroom, or perform a physical task like a squat, lunge, hand movement, or facial gesture. When the music stops, students must freeze.

- **Critical thinking and kinesthetic challenge:** Challenge students to move to the other side of the room without touching the floor using only a jump rope, scooter, and one chair.

While focus-based, brain-centered, and whole-class movement strategies benefit students, teachers may wish to take movement to the next level by pairing it with academic content.

## Content-Oriented

To maximize time and cover academic content that appears on state and national assessments, teachers sometimes disregard strategies that don't target academic outcomes. However, physical activities can incorporate content lessons to meet students' needs for movement and achieve academic outcomes. Although students focus better when they have activity breaks, they access the most significant academic benefits when physical activity is integrated with academic subjects (Egger, Benzing, Conzelmann, & Schmidt, 2019). Researchers David Blazar and Cynthia Pollard (2022) find that teachers who report high levels of student engagement and high test scores often have students collaborating in pairs or groups, using tactile objects to solve problems, or playing games. In addition, research suggests teachers favor this approach (Dinkel, Schaffer, Snyder, & Lee, 2017; Mullins, Michaliszyn, Kelly-Miller, & Groll, 2019).

While it isn't always possible to integrate physical exercise in the classroom in the same way as at the gym or the playground, the best alternative is to integrate student movement while teaching content. Movement integration happens when teachers include physical activity in the general education classroom during normal instructional time (Webster, Russ, Vazou, Goh, & Erwin, 2015).

Consider the following ideas, suitable for all content areas, which may be adjusted to suit various age levels and unique needs.

- Students complete a bell ringer question on the board while standing and sit when finished.

- Students use hand motions and gestures in a song to learn concepts.

- Students establish and use gestures to represent specific concepts, vocabulary terms, or abstract ideas.

- Students participate in virtual and augmented reality simulations such as designing, building, and testing wind turbines or visiting a research station and exploring bacteria in melting water through the use of technology.

- Students answer quick assessments by displaying thumbs up or down, putting arms up to agree or making an *X* with their arms to disagree, or holding up cards (for example, true or false cards, multiple-choice answer cards, or terminology cards).

- Students create review videos as a closure activity on Flip (https://info.flip.com) or a private YouTube channel.

- Students stand until they answer a question posed by the teacher.

- Students record their thinking about specific content on paper, then stand and pair up with another student to compare ideas.

- Students take seven steps in any direction and find a partner to discuss a posted prompt.

- Students form small groups and pass a ball back and forth while each participant states something they learned during the lesson.

- Students play Jenga in groups, answering a question on a review sheet as part of their turn. After the group checks their answer for correctness, a student from that group pulls a block.

- Students respond to statements posted on the board. Students who agree the statement is true perform a jumping jack. Students who believe the statement is false perform a squat.

Consider the following ideas, arranged by content area.

- **Language arts:** The following activities are well-suited to language arts classes and may be adjusted based on students' ages and unique needs.

  - Students jump when the teacher uses a keyword in a sentence.

  - Students perform a jumping jack for each letter when spelling a word.

  - When given punctuation and word cards, students line up in order to make a complete sentence with their cards.

  - Students trace words in dirt, sand, or shaving cream.

  - Students act out a stanza from a poem or key section of a story.

- **Mathematics:** The following activities work well in mathematics classes and may be adjusted based on students' ages and unique needs.

  - Students represent numbers on a number line by walking forward a certain number of steps to show the addition of numbers and backward to represent subtraction.

  - When reviewing the day's calendar, students perform a squat for each day of the month.

  - Students jump to number squares to indicate the correct answer to a mathematics problem.

  - Students search for ten word problems hidden throughout the classroom and then solve them.

  - Students analyze two complex mathematics scenarios completed by their peers. The teacher places the scenarios at opposite ends of the room and instructs students to move to the side of the room containing what they feel is the most accurate solution. Students discuss their rationale with a peer.

- **Science:** The following activities are a good fit for science classes and may be adjusted based on students' ages and unique needs.

  - Students create hand gestures to represent each part of the water cycle.

  - Students conduct a scientific lab with an inquiry activity. For example, students use three different fertilizers and analyze the growth rate of bean plants.

  - Students sit back-to-back and lock their arms with a partner, then the pair attempts to stand up. They analyze how Newton's three laws apply to their situation.

  - Students review key concepts by designing mind maps linking concepts learned in the unit and posting them on the walls around the room.

  - Students move around the room to answer reflection questions posted on the walls about the lab.

- **Social studies:** The following activities are well-suited to social studies classes and may be adjusted based on students' ages and unique needs.

  - Students rotate among stations to analyze case studies involving the U.S. Bill of Rights.

- Students pretend to work as marine archaeologists and dive for artifacts by crawling on the floor to retrieve a card with a picture and description of an item found by early explorers. Students analyze what the images and information reveal about the explorers' motives.

- Students create a puppet show summarizing a historical event.

- Students write new lyrics to a current song that summarizes a historical time period or event and perform the song for their peers.

# Six Key Factors That Drive Engagement

The remaining chapters in the book offer over thirty strategies to help teachers maximize cognitive engagement through thinking tasks that focus on academic content while integrating student movement. What is it about pairing cognitive tasks with movement that creates engagement? Educator Mike Anderson (2021) suggests there are six key intrinsic motivators activated by learning through movement.

1. **Autonomy:** Giving students some power and choice over how they learn is motivating. Teachers may offer students the choice of working alone or with a partner. They may allow students to choose a partner. Another way to support autonomy is giving students choices of assignments. Teachers may offer students several prompts or tasks and allow them to select one to complete. Finally, consider allowing students to choose where they want to work in the class: at their desk, on a bean bag, or at the group table.

2. **Belonging:** One of students' basic needs is to connect with peers. Movement tasks often include conversations with a partner, group, or team, which builds these connections and fosters positive relationships among students.

3. **Competence:** Students want to know that they are growing and getting smarter. Through movement activities that focus on academic content, students expand their understanding and experience greater levels of competence.

4. **Purpose:** When teachers ensure lessons address *why* students are learning the topic or skills, students are more likely to be engaged; they understand the purpose behind the learning. To create an even stronger connection to purpose, use content to support students in addressing real-life problems, such as building a disability ramp for the school gym or creating an advertising campaign for a local business. Lessons can also draw specific connections to the students themselves. Ask students, "How do you feel about this topic?" and facilitate a class discussion. Before beginning a movement activity, articulate the learning's purpose. Student movement tied to a purpose can enhance students' sense that the activity is meaningful.

5. **Fun:** Academic learning does not have to be drudgery! Movement tasks bring excitement and novelty into lessons and spark students' interest in participating in meaningful academic tasks. Intrinsic motivation is more sustainable and powerful than extrinsic motivation. While textbook-based instruction is sometimes a valuable learning experience, incorporating movement can spark students' cognitive interest in academic content.

6. **Curiosity:** Lessons that connect to students' interests and curiosity can spur intrinsic motivation. Students may have a natural tendency to ignore much of what is occurring around them, selectively noticing things that are interesting, novel, or compelling. Movement tasks can introduce a novel element and include thought-provoking questions to challenge students' thinking.

These six key motivating factors drive students' enthusiasm and engagement as teachers integrate student movement. As you read through the strategies in this book and integrate them into your classroom, keep these six factors in mind. Notice whether your use of the strategies embodies these factors and, if not, consider how you might adjust them to do so.

## Discussion Questions

As you reflect on this chapter, consider the following five questions.

1. What active learning strategies do you currently use to optimize learning?

2. What benefits of movement integration do you value most for your students?

3. Based on these concepts, what is your vision for integrating movement into your classroom?

4. How do you see Anderson's (2021) six key motivating factors present (or missing) in your classroom lessons?

5. Which of Anderson's (2021) six key motivating factors could you enhance by incorporating more movement in your classroom?

## Action Steps

Use the following three activities to put this chapter's concepts to work in your own classroom.

1. Choose an idea presented in the chapter and use or adapt it for your classroom.

2. Have a colleague observe your class and suggest ways to enhance student movement in your classroom.

3. Observe a teacher known for successfully integrating student movement and note ways you can adapt their practices in your classroom.

# CHAPTER 3

# Moving in Pairs

*Ms. Markel distributes a chart to each student. The first column contains three questions connected to the class's recent unit on health and the second column contains room for students to write a response. Students work independently to write their answers in the second column. After a designated amount of time, they stand up and pair off. Standing around the room in pairs, students share their responses with their partner and write their partner's responses to each question in the third column of their chart. After finishing their partner discussion, students find a second partner and repeat the process, writing their new partner's responses in the fourth column. Students then return to their seats, and the teacher offers them a few minutes to quietly examine the different perspectives they received from their peers. Ms. Markel facilitates a class discussion, inviting students to explore reasons for the different perspectives.*

What do you notice about Ms. Markel's classroom? What benefits might students be accessing by working in pairs? Would you say that Ms. Markel's students are engaged or disengaged in the learning process?

The instructional model in which the teacher poses recall questions and calls on one student to answer is a model that creates low levels of student engagement. And yet, a large majority of classrooms still rely on this approach. While this method checks for student understanding, it does not engage all students in many of the key ways we've discussed in previous chapters. This approach fails to offer students meaningful discussions, novel learning experiences, opportunities to co-create learning, access to higher-order thinking, and cultural responsiveness.

In contrast, when students learn through collaborative activities—conversing with peers and sharing ideas—they move into higher orders of application and transfer and are more successfully engaged. Teacher instruction still has a place in the classroom, such as establishing foundational context about new content. However, once students have sufficient information about a topic, they can work together in pairs to create connections between those ideas.

In this chapter, I share the benefits of allowing students to work with a partner to discuss teacher-designated questions. I outline the steps you'll need to take to prepare for integrating peer discussions. Finally, I offer you eleven strategies for integrating movement into your classroom via partner conversations.

## Benefits of Working in Pairs

What does it look like for students to work in pairs? Ideal classroom discussions with peers involve thinking aloud, listening to others, questioning, justifying, and exploring (Fisher, Frey, & Hattie, 2020). Focused conversations, in which students state in their own words what they learned and what they want to know, build understanding. These conversations are key to deepening student engagement: they allow students to learn the content while gaining communication and social skills important at every grade level and content area, and important for future employment (Hernandez, 2018).

Instead of learning from the teacher's singular perspective, as happens in lecture-style instruction, collaborative learning offers students access to diverse ideas and perspectives from students with a variety of home cultures. Students can add on another idea, offer additional evidence, or suggest an alternate perspective. These perspectives can lead to thoughtful student critiques and feedback. As students learn in discussions to support their thinking with evidence, students may find themselves revising their ideas based on new information. Another benefit of these partner discussions is they make student learning visible and strengthen the classroom community (Ostroff, 2020).

Research shows that conversations are one of the most effective practices teachers can use in classrooms to promote higher achievement (Hammond, 2020; Hattie, 2012). Education professor John Hattie contends that dialogues between and among peers are a significant way to enhance instruction, with an effect size of 0.82, which represents over two years' worth of growth in one year (Fisher, Frey, & Hattie, 2016). In addition, when students engage in thoughtful discussion about a text, they achieve higher test scores and overall academic achievement (Hoffer, 2020; U.S. Department of Education, 2013). Allowing student discussion is not wasted time; it's an opportunity for students to deepen their understanding of content, leading to positive academic outcomes.

Unfortunately, not all students are able to access the benefits described in the research. Some students need additional support to engage in discussions. Discussion stems are a helpful tool to empower students to effectively participate (U.S. Department of Education, 2013). Figure 3.1 includes examples of discussion stems teachers may provide to students to facilitate conversations with a partner.

| Purpose | Discussion Stems |
|---|---|
| **Affirm** | You made a great point about . . . .<br><br>My ideas build on _____'s idea . . . . |
| **Disagree** | That's a good point, but I think . . . .<br><br>I understand what you're saying. Have you thought about . . . ? |
| **Clarify** | In other words, are you saying . . . ?<br><br>I have a question about . . . .<br><br>Can you explain . . . ? |
| **Connect** | This reminds me of . . . .<br><br>This is similar to . . . . |

**Figure 3.1:** Discussion stems.

*Visit* **go.SolutionTree.com/studentengagement** *for a free reproducible version of this figure.*

Students may need time, practice, and a little coaching to succeed in dialoging with peers. With careful planning, teachers can prepare students to engage in discussion.

# Steps to Prepare for Discussion

Students unaccustomed to collaborative learning will need practice and support to successfully transition to working in pairs. Prepare students to work with peers by establishing context, selecting partners, and posing questions in advance.

## Establish Context

Students may need an opportunity to deepen their understanding of the topic before they're ready to discuss it with a partner. Ask yourself: What do my students need to know to be able to engage in the discussion? Then design a task students can undertake to prepare themselves accordingly, whether that be reading a text, analyzing a graph, or reviewing quotes. If needed, build in a formative assessment to gain feedback on any gaps in student understanding.

For example, imagine a teacher recognizes his students have varying understandings of key terms involved in the upcoming discussion. He assigns students to create a vocabulary notebook (or digital version) that includes each term, a non-linguistic representation of the term, an example, and a non-example. To activate background knowledge and clarify the content, the teacher assigns students to develop a concept map or mind map. He collects the maps as a formative assessment to analyze gaps in understanding. The teacher then uses this formative data to design questions that partners can discuss to address misconceptions.

## Select Partners

Establishing effective discussion groups is important. When considering how to pair students, teachers need to decide whether they'll assign partners or allow students to select their own. When students choose a partner, they sometimes select a friend, which can turn into more of a distraction than a collaboration. However, teachers can set expectations that guide students to choose an appropriate partner. For example, a teacher can instruct students to partner with a person who is a strong organizer or a creative thinker. If the teacher decides to select partner groups for students, the teacher should consider the students' academic strengths, social skills, home cultures, and unique needs to create optimal partnerships. As writer and drama teacher Kerry Hishon (n.d.) notes, there are pros and cons to each approach, so reflect on the implications for your students, choose the method that's best for your class, and set expectations as needed.

If you assign partners, you can communicate the pairs to students in creative ways—as opposed to just calling out names or posting a list—to get them invested in the process. Consider the following creative strategies for communicating partner groups to your class.

- For primary classrooms, give each student a name that is half of a famous pair (for example, Minnie Mouse) and instruct them to find their matching partner.

- For secondary classrooms, provide one partner with the name of a band and instruct them to find the partner with one of the band's song titles.

Consider the following creative approaches to matching random pairs.

- Instruct students to line up in order of shoe size, hair length, number of buttons on clothing, or other criteria. Have students pair up with the person standing beside them.

- Use technology, like Team Shake (www.rhine-o .com/www/iphone-apps/team-shake), to randomly assign students to groups.

- Instruct students to find a partner who shares a criterion of your choice (for example, wearing the same color or has the same middle initial, eye color, or birthday month).

Consider the following creative approaches to allowing students to choose their partners.

- Allow students to sign up to work with a partner of their choice. For example, students might choose three different partners to work with during the week. Inform students that when they make a partner choice, they will record their partner's name on their paper in the numbered spot and the other person will do the same.

- Invite students to select partners by exchanging colored cards. For example, instruct students to select two different partners to work with throughout the week and give each student two cards of different colors (for example, each student receives a red card and a blue card). Students record their name on the card, stand up, and trade their card with another student. Each student will then have two new cards with the names of a red partner and a blue partner.

## Pose Questions

Successful partner discussions are fueled by high-level questions. Develop a list of questions to support partners to engage in higher-order thinking. Focus on creating questions that will ignite students' interest in the topic. Make sure questions are open-ended with no right answer. Some powerful questions teachers can ask during their lessons include the following (Alber, 2013; TeachThought 2022).

- What do you think about _____?

- Why do you think so?

- How do you know _____?

- Can you tell me more about _____?

- What questions do you still have?

- What evidence would you point to that supports (or refutes) _____?

- What is the most important idea? Explain your thinking.

- What are the advantages or disadvantages of _____?

- How does _____ relate to _____?

- What other ideas would you add?

- How would you improve on this design (or idea)?

- What might happen next if _____?

Alternatively, teachers can select a current issue, assign students to develop arguments for and against it, and allow time for debate between partners. You might imagine this can lead to lively discussion. Equip students with the tools they need to conduct a successful debate. One such tool is Brian Stanfield's (2000) ORID protocol for strategic questioning—*objective, reflective, interpretive, decisional.* The ORID protocol allows students to analyze complex topics—such as improving

systems of government, reforming the criminal justice system, or understanding advanced literature—and address real-world problems like climate change (Stanfield, 2000) by exploring the following factors:

- **Objective:** The facts known

- **Reflective:** People's feeling about the topic or what is liked or disliked

- **Interpretive:** The issues or challenges (How might we _____? What if we _____?)

- **Decisional:** The decision or response, which might include a solution with action steps

Figure 3.2 contains a worksheet you can provide students to help them prepare for a debate using the ORID protocol.

As the class becomes accustomed to partner discussions, teachers can hand over more responsibility to students by allowing them to develop their own questions. Many teachers are accustomed to asking students, "Do you have any questions?" and providing a few seconds of thinking time. However, teachers must provide quiet time for students to thoughtfully construct high-level questions. Consider the following strategies to support students in writing analytical questions.

- **Statement and question:** Close class by asking students to identify the most important point of the lesson and construct a corresponding lingering question.

- **Muddiest point:** End class by allowing students to state the most confusing (muddiest) point.

Use the questions and muddy points as the focus of the next day's partner discussion. As you begin discussions, some students will be ready to dive right in while others may need practice and support to become proficient at conversing in pairs. By building new habits over time, teachers and students construct a classroom culture of high-level peer discussion. Ultimately, the suggestions and strategies in this chapter aim to provide flexible tools. You know your classroom and your students better than anyone. Take time to reflect on what you've read and consider the most effective ways to implement these tools in your classroom. The most important thing is to create an environment where students feel they are safe to express themselves and trusted

| Debate Worksheet | | |
| --- | --- | --- |
| **Discussion Level** | **Purpose** | **Questions to Consider** |
| Objective | Establish what facts you know about this topic. | What do you notice?<br><br><br>What do you already know?<br><br><br>What do you still need to know? |
| Reflective | Identify how people feel about this topic, and what people like or dislike about it. | What factors make this topic complex?<br><br><br>Who is affected by this issue? |
| Interpretive | Recognize the issues or challenges that arise around this topic. | What makes this topic controversial? |
| Decisional | Make a decision or choose a response, including appropriate action steps. | What steps do we want to take in response? |

**Figure 3.2:** Preparing for debate using the ORID protocol.

*Visit **go.SolutionTree.com/studentengagement** for a free reproducible version of this figure.*

to co-create their learning. Some specific ways teachers can take action to promote an environment conducive to effective dialogue include the following (Kentucky Department of Education, 2020).

- Posing high-level questions

- Using wait time to allow all students to think and refine their thoughts

- Listening to students' ideas

- Summarizing students' points

- Creating new questions to add to the conversation

- Affirming and supporting students as they expand their understanding

When structured appropriately, partner discussions increase student engagement and critical thinking. To capitalize on the powerful benefits of student discourse, this chapter profiles eleven strategies that utilize partner conversations with movement to challenge students to deeper levels of thinking.

## Strategy 1: Find an Expert

*Find an Expert* enables students to move around the classroom and collaborate with other students, ascertaining others' thoughts on a topic before revisiting their own answers. Students can gain new perspectives as well as notice misconceptions in their peers' answers. As you read in the example of Ms. Markel's class at the beginning of this chapter, *Find an Expert* offers students the benefit of gaining various perspectives by applying learning in a personalized context. To help students with this strategy, provide them a chart like the one in figure 3.3.

. . . . . . . . . . . . . . . . . . . . . . . . . . . . . . . . .

### CLASSROOM EXAMPLE

After conducting an experiment involving chemical changes in science class, a teacher gives students a chart containing two questions, including "What evidence proves this was a chemical change?" After recording their own ideas, students divide into pairs, and share their answers to the questions. Each student writes down their partner's name and answers. The students then move around the classroom and find another partner, repeating the process until their table is complete with all the answers.

. . . . . . . . . . . . . . . . . . . . . . . . . . . . . . . . .

| Question | |
|---|---|
| What evidence proves this was a chemical change? | What is one way you could show a friend that there are chemical changes? |
| **My Answer** | |
| I noticed an odor. Plus, the temperature and color changed. | When you bake a cake, the ingredients are wet at first and then turn solid. |
| **Partner 1 Response** | |
| I smelled an odor. | I played a game where we smashed eggs trying to figure out which ones were hard boiled and which ones were not. Eggs become hard when you boil them. |
| **Partner 2 Response** | |
| I saw the temperature change. | Milk in the refrigerator is liquid, but if I leave it out it gets clumpy. |

**Figure 3.3:** Sample graphic organizer.

*Visit **go.SolutionTree.com/studentengagement** for a free reproducible version of this figure.*

### Strategy Steps

Use the following steps to help you implement the *Find an Expert* strategy.

1. Create a chart (see figure 3.3) for students to use during this activity. Include high-level questions relevant to the lesson.

2. Hand out a chart to each student, and instruct them to record an answer in the space provided.

3. Divide students into pairs, and allow them to share their answer with a partner, then record their partner's name and responses.

4. Have students repeat the process with a second partner.

5. Instruct students to return to their seats and review the responses they collected, revising their initial answers if needed.

6. Facilitate a classroom discussion about students' observations, noticing the diverse perspectives and ideas represented among their peers.

## Variations

You can use the following variations in association with this strategy.

- For younger students, revise the chart to contain only one question.

- Play the icebreaker, *Find Someone Who.* Using either a checklist or bingo card, write down names of television shows, foods, places, sports, and other student interests. Students rotate around the room, finding a person who likes one of the items displayed on the card. Alternatively, allow students to create the prompts that appear in the boxes.

- Try *Partner Up*, in which the teacher distributes a card containing either a word or its definition to each student. Students seek out the partner whose card matches theirs.

- Play *Four More*, instructing students to write down two key ideas they learned in the lesson. Students walk around the classroom, choose four other students to share one of their ideas with, and record one of each partner's ideas.

## Additional Content Area Examples

This section provides examples of ways you can connect this strategy to your teaching in different content areas.

- A language arts teacher provides each student a chart that contains different types of sentences (simple, compound, complex, and compound-complex). Students move around the room, find peers who can identify the types of sentences in each cell of the table, and then justify how they reached that conclusion.

- As a review of bivariate data, a mathematics teacher provides students with a chart that contains examples in each cell of two quantitative categories. Students find a partner, take turns stating what type of correlation the two categories have, and justify their answers. At the end of the activity, students create a new chart with their own examples of *positive, negative,* and *no correlation* and then repeat the process.

- A science teacher projects nine different images (including multicellular and unicellular cells, nucleus, and mitochondria) onto the board and instructs students to identify each cell's type and functions. Students record their responses in a chart. Students then find a peer, compare answers, and justify their responses to further explain the function of that particular cell type or part. Students seek a new partner to discuss each box on their grid.

- After introducing economic terms and explaining the relationship between supply and demand, a social studies teacher instructs students to work with a partner to complete their chart containing real-world scenarios. Students discuss which economics terms apply to each scenario and record their ideas in the chart. Students seek a new partner to complete each scenario in the chart.

- A music teacher instructs students to review their lesson by moving around the classroom and completing a chart identifying various note values and rest values. Students collaborate with a partner to identify the type of note and rest and its value in 4/4 time. Students seek a new partner to complete each box in the chart.

## Differentiated Options

This section provides examples of ways you can modify this strategy for students who need additional support or opportunities to extend their learning.

- Target both low-level and high-level thinking by creating questions at various difficulty levels, including those that ask students to summarize information and compare concepts. These questions provide the foundational information. To challenge students, ask higher-level questions that encourage students to analyze quotes, connect new knowledge to current knowledge, or relate content to real-world situations.

- To support students' diverse social-emotional needs, find creative ways to assign pairs, such as using colors, numbers, or labels on each student's chart, and instruct them to find a partner with a matching paper. This may help students be more at ease as they're developing social skills.

- For students who need more support, give the student a strip of paper with an answer to one of the questions. Instruct the student to find the question that goes with their answer strip.

- Designate a teacher station for students to visit if they need to discuss the topic with the teacher before beginning the activity.

### Strategy 2: Think, Pair, Share Boards

*Think, Pair, Share Boards* provides students time to think individually about a topic; it then asks them to compare their thinking with other students, refine their answers, and display their answers. Teachers often ask high-level thinking questions and expect students to answer without adequate time. This strategy allows students time to cultivate and refine their thinking before sharing with the entire class.

. . . . . . . . . . . . . . . . . . . . . . . . . . . . . . . . . . . .

### CLASSROOM EXAMPLE

A mathematics teacher gives students information about a hypothetical room: its dimensions, the cost of materials and labor, and the time needed to paint the room. The teacher asks how much paint is required to paint the room. Once students calculate the answer at their desk, they pair off and obtain a dry-erase board. Students stand with their partners, discuss their calculations, and agree on the correct answer. The pairs sit and record their answer on their boards. The teacher asks students to raise their boards to show their answers. Seeing that only some of the students have completed the calculation correctly, the teacher facilitates a classroom discussion to clear up misunderstandings.

. . . . . . . . . . . . . . . . . . . . . . . . . . . . . . . . . . . .

#### Strategy Steps

Use the following steps to help you implement the *Think, Pair, Share Boards* strategy.

1. Pose a problem or question to the students.

2. Allow students to write down their answers at their desk.

3. Divide the class into pairs and give each pair a dry-erase board and marker.

4. Instruct students to discuss their answers with their partners while standing. When a pair agrees upon an answer, they should sit and record their answer on the dry-erase board.

5. Invite students to raise their boards to show their answers.

6. If there are incorrect answers, address any misunderstandings.

#### Variations

You can use the following variations in association with this strategy.

- Write or project questions on the board to support learners in primary grades or when the questions are especially complex for secondary students.

- Try *Think, Pair, Share, Square* by instructing students to merge with another pair to compare answers once they've recorded their responses.

- Use this strategy as a review game with students individually or in partner groups. Ask review questions, allow time for students to write their responses, then invite students to stand and show their boards. Some teachers allow students to stand up on their chairs.

- Allow students to work with a different partner for each question. After each question, the pair groups change so students have a new partner for each question.

- Lead the class in *Showdown* (Kagan, Kagan, & Kagan, 2016), in which students answer the questions individually then use a thumbs-up gesture as a signal to a partner when they are finished. Partners then share their answers to verify they are correct.

- Instruct students to write several challenging questions based on the lesson. Allow them to work with a partner to compare their questions and select the one they feel is most relevant or will incite effective peer debate. Partners record their best question on their board to share during the whole-class discussion.

#### Additional Content Area Examples

This section provides examples of ways you can connect this strategy to your teaching in different content areas.

- Reviewing ethos, logos, and pathos, a language arts teacher displays a quote on the board and asks students to conclude whether the quote is an ethical appeal, a logical appeal, or an emotional appeal, and then justify their answers. After recording their answers on paper, the students form pairs and discuss their conclusions while standing. After discussing, the students sit and write their answers on their dry-erase boards. Pairs hold their boards overhead so the whole class can review them.

- A mathematics teacher instructs students to draw a model in order to solve a story problem. Students first draw their models on paper and then meet in pairs to display and explain their models. Partners decide which model is best and prepare their reasoning to share with the class.

- A chemistry teacher asks students to convert grams to moles. After students complete the calculation independently, they divide into pairs, discuss their work while standing, and justify their process. Once partners agree on the answer, they sit and record their work on the dry-erase boards to show the class.

- A social studies teacher presents a real-world scenario regarding First Amendment rights. Working individually, students think about what court cases a lawyer might use to argue the case. Then students stand with a partner to identify the most important court cases to cite. Students list the cases on the dry-erase board and present their rationale during a class discussion.

- The teacher of a senior pharmacy-technician course gives students calculations of medications to solve. Students work independently to complete the calculations before standing with a partner to check their work. Once the students agree on an answer, they sit and record their response on their dry-erase board. The teacher asks students to raise their boards to display their answers.

### Differentiated Options

This section provides examples of ways you can modify this strategy for students who need additional support or opportunities to extend their learning.

- Pair students strategically to represent diverse abilities. For example, pair a student with strong verbal skills with a student who prefers the role of scribe.

- Allow students who are reluctant to speak aloud to record their answers digitally in a variety of ways (for example, by recording a video of their answer or taking a photograph of their board) using tools like Flip or Padlet (https://padlet.com).

- For students who need academic assistance, provide supports such as *ask a friend*, *check an online resource*, or *remove a choice* (in the case of working with a multiple-choice question).

## Strategy 3: Line Up, Pair Up

*Line Up, Pair Up* incorporates student movement in pairs in an organized method and encourages opportunities to collaborate with various peers and experience multiple perspectives.

### CLASSROOM EXAMPLE

A teacher informs students that they are to be financial advisers and gives them copies of a family's checkbook register. Each checkbook register displays deposits and expenses along with a daily account balance. The teacher asks students to determine whether the family has enough money to go on a vacation, according to their desired budget. Once students analyze the register and independently determine their recommendation, the teacher instructs them to bring their work and form two parallel lines so that each student stands across from a partner. Students share with their partner the steps they used to solve the problem. Then, the other partner shares any differences in the way they solved the problem.

### Strategy Steps

Use the following steps to help you implement the *Line Up, Pair Up* strategy.

1. Identify the question that students will discuss.

2. Instruct students to form parallel lines facing each other.

3. Designate which line will begin, and establish a time frame for conversation. After the first line of students has shared information, their partners can add on any other ideas related to the question.

4. When the time is up, instruct one of the lines of students to shift three spots to the right, with students at the end of the line returning to the beginning of the line, creating new partners.

5. Repeat the process by asking another question.

### Variations

You can use the following variations in association with this strategy.

- Move the activity outside or to a hallway if more space is needed.

- Use the activity as an icebreaker, providing students with conversation prompts like those included in figure 3.4.

- Play music to cue students to move down to create a new pair, such as in a conga line dance (Vogt & Echevarria, 2007).

### Additional Content Area Examples

This section provides examples of ways you can connect this strategy to your teaching in different content areas.

- A language arts teacher instructs students to create two parallel lines facing one another so that everyone has a partner. The teacher poses a question related to William Golding's *Lord of the Flies*: "What does the conch shell represent, and what is Golding communicating through the use of the conch shell as a symbol?" Students discuss this question with the person across from them. After a few minutes of discussion, one line of students shifts to form new pairs, and the teacher states another discussion question.

- A mathematics teacher guides students to form two parallel lines to find partners. She gives students a number and instructs them to name multiples of the number, in any order they wish. The first student in the pair names as many multiples as they can; when they run out of responses, the other partner takes a turn. Students repeat the activity, this time naming the multiples in order and alternating each response with their partner until they can't name any more multiples or the time runs out.

- A science teacher names a plant (or animal). Students write down an adaptation the organism has acquired and what events contributed to the adaptation. Students form two parallel lines to create partners, and then they discuss their answers in pairs.

| Get to Know You Prompts |
|---|
| What is on your bucket list? |
| Describe someone who inspires you. |
| Describe an experience that changed your life. |
| Describe something you are good at and why. |
| Explain what a perfect day for you would be. |
| Describe a kindness a friend has shown you recently. |
| Given the choice of anyone in the world, whom would you want as a dinner guest? |
| For what in your life do you feel most grateful? |
| If you could wake up tomorrow having gained any one quality or ability, what would it be? |
| What is the greatest accomplishment of your life? |
| What is your most treasured memory? |
| What can you do today that you were not capable of a year ago? |
| Where would you most like to go and why? |
| Would you rather live for a week in the past or the future? |
| How would you describe your future in three words? |

**Figure 3.4:** Icebreaker prompts.

*Visit **go.SolutionTree.com/studentengagement** for a free reproducible version of this figure.*

- A social studies teacher asks students to discuss the causes and effects of imperialism between 1750 and 1900. Students work independently to write their responses on paper. Then, they line up in two parallel lines to form discussion pairs and share their answers with their partner. Afterward, their partner shares their ideas. With extra time available, students collaborate to identify alternative viewpoints on this topic.

- A music teacher asks students to discuss the origins of blues music in the United States. Students work independently and record their responses on paper, then form two parallel lines to find partners and take turns sharing their responses in pairs.

### Differentiated Options

This section provides examples of ways you can modify this strategy for students who need additional support or opportunities to extend their learning.

- For students who need additional academic support, prepare questions ahead of time and provide a handout to students they can use to record notes from the discussion.

- To support different interests, allow students to discuss a prompt of their choice with their partners.

- For additional academic support, provide students with a word bank to remind them of key terms connected to the discussion topic.

## Strategy 4: Circle Around

*Circle Around* provides students the opportunity to collaborate with a peer while integrating movement and incorporating music.

### CLASSROOM EXAMPLE

In music class, students are learning about melody, rhythm, harmony, tempo, dynamics, and timbre. The teacher hands out a sheet with questions and divides the class into two groups, instructing students to form an exterior and interior circle. The teacher plays the music, and students rotate in a circular motion in opposite directions. When the music stops, students find the closest partner in the other circle and discuss the first question on their handout: "How would you describe the melody of this song?" As students conclude their discussion, the teacher plays the music again, and students rotate around the circle until the music stops. Students discuss the second question with their new partner: "How is the rhythm in this song different from that of the 'Happy Birthday' song?"

### Strategy Steps

Use the following steps to help you implement the *Circle Around* strategy.

1. Create a handout with high-level questions that review concepts or debrief from an experience (for example, a video, experiment, or reading).

2. Distribute the handout to all students and divide the class in half, instructing one group to make a large exterior circle and the other group to make a smaller interior circle.

3. Play music, and cue students to walk around the circle until the music stops; ensure the interior circle moves in a clockwise motion and the exterior circle moves in a counterclockwise motion. Select appropriate music that students enjoy.

4. When the music stops, students form pairs with the person across from them. Allow students to discuss the first question on the handout.

5. Repeat the process to create new pairs that will discuss the next question on the handout.

### Variations

You can use the following variations in association with this strategy.

- Project questions on a screen instead of distributing a handout to students.

- Allow students to record their answers on paper after discussing with their partners. Provide materials (such as a clipboard or dry-erase board as needed).

### Additional Content Area Examples

This section provides examples of ways you can connect this strategy to your teaching in different content areas.

- A language arts teacher prepares a handout with discussion questions about how the character developments of Scout, Jem, and Atticus convey the main themes in Harper Lee's *To Kill A Mockingbird*. After receiving the handout, students form two circles. While music plays, the outside circle rotates clockwise while the inside circle rotates counterclockwise. When the music stops, students form pairs with the opposing circle and answer the first question. Students repeat the process until they have discussed each question on the handout.

- A mathematics teacher divides the students and instructs them to form two circles. The teacher assigns each circle a designated value—the inner circle has the number 2 and the outer circle has the number 3—and instructs students to move in opposite directions while the music plays. When the music stops, students pair up and simplify a given expression on the board using their number for a blank space or variable. Partners state their equation and discuss how to arrive at an answer. When the students rotate, the teacher displays a new expression and students repeat the process. At the end of the activity, the teacher leads a discussion about how the inner circle's answers typically compared to the outer circle's answers. The class also discusses common mistakes and difficulties they faced while making the calculations.

- A science class reviews cell division by reading statements and viewing images that require students to apply and analyze information to derive an answer. The teacher reads a statement that asks students to describe in their own words the significance of the process of mitosis. Students form two circles and rotate in opposite directions while the teacher plays music. When the music stops, students discuss their ideas with the partner closest to them in the opposite circle. Students repeat this process, this time examining images of living human cells projected on the screen and identifying the stage of mitosis.

- A social studies teacher leads students in a review of migration and how human interactions affect and influence cultures. The teacher asks students to identify new goods from other countries that have emerged in their community and how these goods positively enhance diversity. Students form two circles and rotate in opposite directions while the teacher plays music. When the music stops, students discuss their ideas with the partner closest to them in the opposite circle.

- A teacher reviews art elements by showing different pieces of art and asking students to apply their understanding to analyze the art piece. Students form two circles and rotate in opposite directions while the teacher plays music. The teacher displays the 1931 painting *Fall Plowing* by Grant Wood and asks students to identify elements in the piece with the person across from them.

### Differentiated Options

This section provides examples of ways you can modify this strategy for students who need additional support or opportunities to extend their learning.

- Provide discussion stems to aid students who need academic assistance or social skills support in conversing with their partner.

- Allow students to draw or act out their responses. Partners can guess what the response means.

## Strategy 5: Musical Mingle

While the previous two strategies included the teacher essentially designating partners, in *Musical Mingle* students move around the classroom and choose a partner nearby, giving them more voice in selecting partners. Like the previous strategy, students typically enjoy a burst of music in the classroom. To boost student interest, select appropriate music that represents their favorite tunes. Teachers may also share their favorite tunes with the class to provide variety and build a personal connection.

### CLASSROOM EXAMPLE

A science teacher composes discussion questions on the board based on quantitative and qualitative data. As the teacher plays music, students move around the room. When the music stops, students find a partner closest to them and discuss whether the question represents qualitative or quantitative data. They discuss their opinions and support their claims with content learned in class. Once the students finish discussing, the teacher plays the music again, and the process repeats. The activity continues until students discuss the last question.

• • • • • • • • • • • • • • • • • • • • • • • • • • • • • • • • • •

### Strategy Steps

Use the following steps to help you implement the *Musical Mingle* strategy.

1. Create discussion questions based on content learned in class and select music you will play for this activity.

2. Instruct students to meander around the room until the music stops.

3. When the music stops, students pair up with the peer standing closest to them and discuss a designated question.

4. Repeat the process until students have discussed the last question.

### Variations

You can use the following variations in association with this strategy.

- Instead of stopping the music, allow it to continue and instruct students to share their answer with as many partners as possible before the music ends. In this case, select instrumental music so students can focus on the conversations.

- Instead of instructing students to pair off immediately, provide time for them to think on their own. Perhaps play different music during this think time so that when the tune changes, students know to find their partner. In this case, make sure the music does not include words. After the think time music stops, the teacher could select a few partner groups to share their answers aloud with the class.

### Additional Content Area Examples

This section provides examples of ways you can connect this strategy to your teaching in different content areas.

- A language arts teacher tells students they are going to deepen their understanding of poetic techniques and devices used in Edgar Allan Poe's "The Raven" by discussing it with a partner. Students move around the room as the teacher plays music. When the music stops, students pair up with the person closest to them. The teacher displays a line from the poem, and students are tasked with identifying the poetic technique or device used in the line.

- To review a recent lesson, a mathematics teacher plays music and instructs students to walk around the room. When the music stops, students pair up with the person closest to them. The teacher names a category such as *prime numbers, words used for adding,* or *three-dimensional shapes.* Partners try to name as many of these as they can during the given time. The teacher celebrates the pair who notes the most ideas in each category.

- A science teacher tasks students with answering a list of discussion questions. Students move around the room while the teacher plays music. When the music stops, students pair up with the person closest to them and discuss, for example, why air and water are important for plant survival and growth. Students continue the activity until they answer all the discussion questions.

- After completing a lesson about leaders in the ancient world, a social studies teacher plays music for students to mingle around the room. When the music stops, students pair up with the person closest to them and discuss the most significant accomplishment of the leader identified by the teacher, supporting their argument with historical evidence.

- An art teacher projects an image of a sculpture on the board as the music plays and students move around the classroom. When the music stops, students pair up with the person closest to them and discuss what techniques the artist used to create the piece. The teacher repeats the process, displaying a new piece of art.

### Differentiated Options

This section provides examples of ways you can modify this strategy for students who need additional support or opportunities to extend their learning.

- To support students who might need to read the question several times before commenting, post discussion questions around the room.

- Allow students who need more time to generate their ideas to brainstorm answers to the prompt independently before sharing with their partner.

## Strategy 6: Solve and Switch

*Solve and Switch* is a perfect strategy for practicing application skills. Students can check science or mathematics computations, identify figurative language in a short passage, correct grammar mistakes, or revise a thesis statement. This is a great activity for getting students moving around the room, interacting with peers, and applying their knowledge and skills.

. . . . . . . . . . . . . . . . . . . . . . . . . . . . .

### CLASSROOM EXAMPLE

While learning about addition in a mathematics class, each student receives an addition word problem about pizza. The word problems include irrelevant numbers alongside useful information to challenge students to identify the necessary components for solving the problem. Students work out the answer on paper, find a partner, and then switch papers. Partners share their answers and explain how they solved the equation. If they agree on an answer, they move on and find a new partner; if they disagree, they try to find the reason for their different answers.

. . . . . . . . . . . . . . . . . . . . . . . . . . . . .

### Strategy Steps

Use the following steps to help you implement the *Solve and Switch* strategy.

1. Create a review sheet with ten or more questions depending on the size of the class. These can be application questions that allow students to practice skills but may also include more cognitively demanding tasks such as analyzing passages or scenarios.

2. Print copies of the review sheets and cut them into sections so that each strip contains one

question. Alternatively, write each question on a note card.

3. Pass out a question strip or note card to each student, and instruct students to answer their question.

4. Ask students to stand up and move around the room to find a partner with a different question.

5. Instruct students to switch questions, solve their partner's questions, and discuss their answers and rationale. If the partners disagree on the answer, ask them to work together to arrive at the correct answer and raise their hands if they need support. If the partners agree on the answer to both questions, they will take the new question they solved and find another partner.

6. Repeat the activity until students have answered most of the questions.

### Variations

You can use the following variations in association with this strategy.

- Write the definition or answer to the review question on the back of each sheet or card. Students cue their partner to solve the question, not allowing them to see the answer. If they answer the question correctly, their partner praises them. If they answer incorrectly, their partner coaches them through the problem. Students switch roles, then move on to a new partner.

- Try *Quiz-Quiz-Trade* (Kagan et. al, 2016). Students create a question card based on what they have learned, then stand up and find a partner. One partner shares their question and the other student provides an answer. If the student is incorrect, the questioner gives clues. Then, they reverse roles. Once the partners have both answered the questions, they trade question cards and find a new partner, repeating the process.

### Additional Content Area Examples

This section provides examples of ways you can connect this strategy to your teaching in different content areas.

- A language arts teacher provides each student with a slip of paper containing a vocabulary word from that week's lesson on one side and the definition on the other. Once classmates assemble into pairs, one student presents the side with the definition while the other student tries to guess the vocabulary term. Once each partner has guessed the term, they swap slips and find another partner to quiz.

- Mathematics students review operations with fractions by receiving a card with a fractions problem and working the problem on their card. Once finished, students stand up and raise their hands until they find a partner. Each student answers the question on the other person's card and then they trade cards. Students put up their hands to signal they're ready for another partner. The backs of the cards include suggested questions or phrases to help students coach their partner. For example, "Do you need a common denominator to solve this?" or "Is the fraction in its simplest form?"

- An advanced science class is studying the digestive system. Students receive cards with questions pertaining to digestive system organs, processes, chemicals, and functions. The students answer the questions on their cards and then find a partner. They answer their partner's questions and then check each other's answers and switch cards. This process continues until every card has been discussed and answered.

- A social studies teacher creates cards containing questions and scenarios about the U.S. government's system of checks and balances. One student's card poses a scenario about a Supreme Court justice accusing members of the U.S. Congress of abusing their authority by using the franking system to send political letters for free. The teacher charges students with deciding what the court can do about this. Students record their ideas and then pair with a partner to discuss available legal options to address the situation.

- To review rhythm counting, a music teacher gives students cards with four measures of music. In pairs, students clap their assigned rhythm for their partner, and the partner checks to make sure it is correct. The students then reverse roles so both students perform the task. After a designated amount of time, the teacher plays music to cue students to trade cards and find a new partner. This process continues until all rhythms have been performed.

### Differentiated Options

This section provides examples of ways you can modify this strategy for students who need additional support or opportunities to extend their learning.

- Provide a randomized list of the answers to students in need of support. Students identify the correct answer from among the available options.

- Make extension questions available beneath the primary question for students who need a more challenging exercise.

## Strategy 7: Ranking

*Ranking* focuses on high-level processes as students evaluate information and determine the best idea, strongest proposal, best mathematical solution, or most effective form of government. Students move the ideas around on their workspace to create the ranking, an activity that appeals to students who prefer kinesthetic learning. To help them with this strategy, provide students with a worksheet such as the one in figure 3.5 (page 38).

• • • • • • • • • • • • • • • • • • • • • • • • • • • •
### CLASSROOM EXAMPLE

Students read an article about key points to consider when selecting a career. Each student underlines the five most important ideas in the article. Students form pairs and discuss the importance of their statements. Each pair develops consensus on the five most important ideas and writes each idea on a separate piece of paper. Pairs then rank the importance of each of the five ideas by moving the papers around to display their rankings. Pairs move around the classroom to view the rankings of other groups. In a classroom discussion, students share similarities and differences between the rankings and whether their thinking changed after viewing others' ideas.
• • • • • • • • • • • • • • • • • • • • • • • • • • • •

| Rank Your Items Worksheet | | |
|---|---|---|
| | Idea | Rationale |
| 1 | Talents | *I think I should select a career that displays my talents. I am good at organizing and working with other students.* |
| 2 | Being with people | *When I choose a career, it should be one that involves being around other people. I like to talk.* |
| 3 | Interesting | *I want a career that is interesting and that challenges me. I do not want to do something that is boring and repetitive.* |
| 4 | Working hours | *My parents work late hours and miss some of my sports events. I want a job that does not require me to work night hours.* |
| 5 | Salary | *I want a career that pays enough money for me to live well, but I do not have to be rich. I can be happy without a lot of money.* |

**Figure 3.5:** Sample worksheet for ranking items in order of importance.

*Visit* **go.SolutionTree.com/studentengagement** *for a free reproducible version of this figure.*

### Strategy Steps

Use the following steps to help you implement the *Ranking* strategy.

1. Identify a reading related to your learning objective.

2. Instruct students to read the source and underline five key sentences.

3. Divide students into pairs and instruct them to compare their underlined statements, agree upon the five most important statements, and record each statement on a separate piece of paper.

4. Ask students to discuss the order of importance of each statement, arrange the papers in order of importance, and record the final order on a sheet of paper along with their rationale.

5. Invite students to move around the classroom and view other groups' rankings.

6. Facilitate a classroom conversation in which students share similarities and differences in the rankings and discuss whether they would change their rankings after viewing other groups' ideas.

### Variations

You can use the following variations in association with this strategy.

- Ask students to debate at the end of the activity, with each pair defending their rankings.

- Have students rate evidence as to its level of importance in supporting the claim.

- Instruct students to develop scoring criteria for an assignment and order the criteria from least important to most important.

### Additional Content Area Examples

This section provides examples of ways you can connect this strategy to your teaching in different content areas.

- A language arts teacher assigns students an informational text, and instructs them to underline five sentences that best convey its central idea. After reading and annotating the article, students find a partner and discuss the five sentences they underlined. Students debate the importance of each sentence, rank them from most important to least important, and record them on a worksheet along with a rationale.

- A mathematics teacher assigns students to solve a multi-step equation and show their work. The teacher then selects five students' works and anonymously displays each one, labeled with a number from one to five. In some of the samples, a few of the steps shown are incorrect or only partially correct. The teacher divides students into pairs, giving each pair number cards from one to five. Students manipulate the cards to rank the work in order from best to least effective strategy and record their reasoning.

- A science teacher shows students a video of a science investigation and provides them a set of cards listing potential conclusions based on the investigation, along with a set of cards with inaccurate conclusions. Working independently, students select the cards they believe are accurate and inaccurate conclusions. Then, students work in pairs to discuss their conclusions and rank their cards to show the best and worst conclusions.

- A social studies teacher assigns students to read the U.S. Declaration of Independence and underline five sentences they believe are the most important. In pairs, students rank the sentences in order of importance and record them on a worksheet along with their rationale.

- A health teacher tasks students with reading an article on heart disease from the American Heart Association about heart-healthy exercises and heart-healthy foods. Students underline five sentences they believe are the most important then work in pairs to rank the sentences in order of importance, discussing their rationale.

### Differentiated Options

This section provides examples of ways you can modify this strategy for students who need additional support or opportunities to extend their learning.

- For an additional challenge, allow students to decide which fact or piece of information could be removed because it is the least important. For example, students can decide which of the first ten amendments to the U.S. Constitution is least important to ensuring individual freedom.

- For visually challenged students, create a whole-group visual representation of the rankings. Post a large chart at the front of the classroom with the numbers one through five, and instruct students to write or tape their statement ranking in each column. If the ranking is numerical, provide students colored stickers or sticky notes for indicating their ranking.

- To support students who have difficulty writing their responses, allow students to make an audio recording of their responses or reflections from the peer-to-peer conversations using a web-based platform like Vocaroo (https://vocaroo.com).

## Strategy 8: Make a Model

While modeling clay (such as Play-Doh) might be viewed as a tool for elementary students, there are many ways to use it to engage students of all ages in high-level thinking. With *Make a Model*, students use modeling clay to visually represent their understanding of concepts. This strategy is great for students who relish kinesthetic tasks. As instructional coach Jane A. G. Kise (2021) notes in *Doable Differentiation*: "At their best, these students use acute observations of the real world to solve problems. They think by touching, manipulating, and experimenting, often through purposeful trial and error" (p. 18). Modeling clay can engage students in a cognitively demanding way because it allows them to create metaphors through sculpture.

### CLASSROOM EXAMPLE

After reviewing plot diagrams, students in a language arts class draw a plot diagram on their desks with a dry-erase marker. Then, working in pairs, students use modeling clay to create objects that represent key elements in the rising action, climax, and falling action in the story *Hatchet* by Gary Paulsen. Students walk around to view one another's representations. After the activity, students stand by the representation they like best and explain why they feel it's the most effective one.

### Strategy Steps

Use the following steps to help you implement the *Make a Model* strategy.

1. Decide what topic students will focus on when they use the modeling clay to symbolize information.

2. Divide students into pairs and instruct them to use the modeling clay to construct models that represent the information.

3. Allow students to examine the other representations throughout the room. Then instruct them

to stand by the representation they feel best represents the concept and invite them to share why they chose it.

### Variations

You can use the following variations in association with this strategy.

- Instruct students to create a clay sculpture that represents a concept. Students walk around, holding their sculpture and sharing with others how it illustrates the idea.

- Instead of using modeling clay, provide students with pipe cleaners or a bag of assorted materials (such as tape, paper, paper clips, straws, and markers) to complete this activity.

- Give students sticky notes and invite them to leave feedback on the work as they circulate around the room to examine other students' thinking.

### Additional Content Area Examples

This section provides examples of ways you can connect this strategy to your teaching in different content areas.

- When discussing direct and indirect characterization in John Steinbeck's *Of Mice and Men*, students in a language arts class partner together to create representations of an assigned character (such as George, Lennie, Curley, Curley's wife, Slim, Candy, Crooks, or Carlson) using modeling clay. Students host an art show where their classmates rotate around the classroom examining the clay figures. The creators explain how their figure accurately represents their assigned character, citing textual evidence.

- A mathematics teacher instructs students to create a three-dimensional solid out of modeling clay with their partners. When the teacher calls a property, such as "more than five vertices," classmates stand by the model they believe best displays that property. Students discuss their reasoning with the classmates who chose their model. The teacher invites a few from each group to defend their choice.

- After learning about different climates in various regions in the world, students in a science class select their favorite animal and identify which climate region would be the best habitat for it. Students use modeling clay to represent the climate region and write down reasons why this climate region is best for their animals. After creating models, students walk around each representation and written justification and stand by the one they believe best displays and explains the reasoning for the selected climate region.

- After introducing U.S. President Roosevelt's federal agencies during the Great Depression, a social studies teacher pairs students and instructs them to select the agency that made the most impact on society at the time. The student pairs create a modeling clay sculpture to represent the agency's impact and develop a written argument to support their decision. Pairs mingle around the classroom sharing their sculpture and justifications. At the end of the activity, the class votes to decide which sculpture best represents the agency.

- After introducing historical music time periods including Renaissance, Baroque, Classical, Romantic, and 20th century music, a music teacher assigns students to listen to a short excerpt of music from each period and create an object with modeling clay that represents that period of music. For example, one student creates an ornate tennis shoe to represent the Baroque period.

### Differentiated Options

This section provides examples of ways you can modify this strategy for students who need additional support or opportunities to extend their learning.

- For students who need an additional challenge, assign them to use the modeling clay to sculpt a metaphor. For example, a student crafts a trophy inscribed with "Good Wins" to represent the theme of good versus evil from a novel they're reading.

- To allow more creativity and challenge, instruct each student in the pair to design a model after they brainstorm ideas together.

- Allow a student with a sensory processing disorder to draw or write about their thinking.

## Strategy 9: Snowstorm

What student hasn't wanted to throw paper in class? *Snowstorm* encourages students to form their own ideas while also considering their classmates' thoughts. This strategy has students standing most of the time while also refining their thinking as they consider diverse ideas and perspectives.

· · · · · · · · · · · · · · · · · · · · · · · · · · · · · · · ·
### CLASSROOM EXAMPLE

After learning about North American westward expansion in social studies, students write three important points they learned about the topic on a piece of paper. Students wad up their paper to create a *snowball* and throw it high in the air in a random direction. The teacher instructs students to stand up, choose one of the snowballs, and move to the perimeter of the classroom. Students silently read the idea written inside the snowball and think of another idea tightly connected to it. The teacher facilitates a discussion in which students share the idea written on their snowball and compare it to their additional connections.
· · · · · · · · · · · · · · · · · · · · · · · · · · · · · · · ·

### Strategy Steps

Use the following steps to help you implement the *Snowstorm* strategy.

1. Ask students to write down the three most important points learned in the lesson.

2. Instruct students to wad up their paper and throw their snowball in the air.

3. Ask students to pick up a snowball, move to the perimeter of the class, and find a partner.

4. Have students individually read the response to themselves and select one important idea the author wrote. Then ask students to think of one new idea they could add.

5. Invite pairs to share their statements and new ideas with their partner.

6. Select a student to begin sharing their statement and providing an additional idea. Rotate in a clockwise pattern around the classroom to let everyone share.

### Variations

You can use the following variations in association with this strategy.

· Invite students to record the most confusing point or a question they have from the lesson.

· Allow students to work with a partner to create their statements.

· For a review game, ask students to write questions on red paper and answers on white paper. Students could then throw their paper snowballs. In pairs, students find a question snowball and a corresponding answer snowball.

· As a lesson summary, invite students to write two truths and a lie on their snowball. As students read their classmates' snowballs, they try to identify the incorrect statement.

### Additional Content Area Examples

This section provides examples of ways you can connect this strategy to your teaching in different content areas.

· After a teaching a lesson on the historical context, both Elizabethan and ancient Roman, for William Shakespeare's *Julius Caesar*, a language arts teacher instructs students to write down three ways the historical information aids them in understanding the play. Students crumple their paper snowballs and toss them into the air; then, students retrieve a random response from the ground and read it. Pairing up, the students choose one of the three statements on which to elaborate and discuss the response with their partners.

· After conducting a lesson about adding fractions, a mathematics teacher assigns students to choose three fraction problems to solve—one of which they should solve incorrectly. Students make their snowballs and throw them in the air. Each student picks up a paper and checks the work, trying to identify the problem worked incorrectly. Pairs check each other's work and then select one problem to work out in front of the class.

· A science teacher instructs students to write down three important details they learned in a lesson about photosynthesis. Then, they wad their paper snowball up and throw it into the air. Students pick up one of the snowballs and independently read the three details. After coming up with a new idea they could add, the student shares their original responses and new ideas with a partner.

- A social studies teacher gives a lesson on the U.S. Declaration of Independence then instructs students to write down three of the lesson's most important points. Once everyone has finished, students throw their snowballs into the air. Each student picks a new snowball and reads the three points. Students brainstorm arguments to support one of the points, then find a partner to share their key point and argument.

- After learning about balancing a checkbook, writing checks, using credit, and incurring debt, students in a family and consumer science class write down three different ideas they learned that will help them be better with their finances. After throwing their snowballs in the air, each student picks up other snowballs, reads the points written, and determines whether there are similarities or differences between the ideas. They then discuss their similarities and differences with a partner.

### Differentiated Options

This section provides examples of ways you can modify this strategy for students who need additional support or opportunities to extend their learning.

- Provide a list of the lesson's key points to any student who needs additional support or scaffolding.

- Allow students who need additional support to use sentence frames (for example, "Because the character _____, I predict she

will _____") to assist in formulating their ideas.

- Invite students who have difficulty writing to create a visual representation of the information they learned.

## Strategy 10: Confer, Compare, and Clarify

*Confer, Compare, and Clarify* encourages students to work with a partner to compare their notes and clarify any misunderstandings (Himmele & Himmele, 2011). Students engage in summarizing, which helps them deepen their understanding. As students compare their notes with others, they can identify information they need to add to their notes along with any lingering questions. To help them with this strategy, provide students a worksheet like the one in figure 3.6.

### CLASSROOM EXAMPLE

The students in a science class watch *All About Body Bacteria!* by Operation Ouch. After watching the video, the students record in their notes what they learned about bacteria and its connection to cheese. The teacher instructs students to stand up with their notes and a pencil or pen and take seven steps in any direction, finding a partner. Each partner shares what they believe is the main point of the video. Then, the partners review each other's notes and record any points their partner mentioned that they missed. The partner group then discusses any questions they still have about bacteria. The pairs take their questions and merge with another pair to discuss them further.

| Notes Worksheet | | |
|---|---|---|
| **My Notes** | **My Partner's Notes** | **Unanswered Questions** |
| My body has bacteria to keep me healthy. Body bacteria and cheese bacteria are somewhat similar. Some of the body cheese smelled really bad. | There are good and bad bacteria. Cheese has lots of bacteria. | Can I not take a bath for a week to conduct a test on bacteria? Can you make things other than cheese with body bacteria? What do I have that probably has the most bacteria? |

**Figure 3.6:** Sample notetaking worksheet.

*Visit **go.SolutionTree.com/studentengagement** for a free reproducible version of this figure.*

### Strategy Steps

Use the following steps to help you implement the *Confer, Compare, and Clarify* strategy.

1. Allow students to take notes on a lecture, reading, or video.

2. Instruct students to stand up, walk seven steps in any direction with their notes and a pen or pencil, and pair up with a student nearest their new location.

3. Have partners confer for a predetermined number of minutes while sharing the most important idea in the lecture, reading, or video.

4. Ask students to silently read their partner's notes and compare them to their own, updating their notes to include any important ideas or information their partner mentioned that they did not record.

5. To clarify, ask pairs to record any questions they have on what they learned, or if they do not have any questions, to think of a thoughtful response based on what they learned.

6. Merge pair groups into groups of four to share and discuss the questions. The teachers should move among the groups, making sure all questions were fully addressed.

### Variations

You can use the following variation in association with this strategy.

- Allow students to post their questions by writing them on a sticky note and putting them on the board or by recording them on a digital board like Padlet (https://padlet.com) or Jamboard (https://bit.ly/3b69B6J), to be discussed as a whole class.

### Additional Content Area Examples

This section provides examples of ways you can connect this strategy to your teaching in different content areas.

- During a unit about Charlotte Brontë's *Jane Eyre*, a language arts teacher assigns students to take notes while watching a video about gothic literature. Once finished, students pair with a partner and compare their notes, adding any important information they missed. Students then write down questions regarding the text and gothicism and discuss the questions with their partners.

- After providing foundational information and allowing students to take notes on constructing exponential functions, a mathematics teacher instructs students to stand and pair up with a partner. They switch notes and silently read them. They switch back and add to their notes additional ideas their partner listed. Together, the pairs write down questions they have about the concept. If they do not have any questions, students create exponential function problems for their classmates to solve.

- After watching and taking notes on a video about matter and energy in organisms, students in a science class pair up and confer. Students then read each other's notes and add anything they may not have written down. Pairs will then find another pair to discuss and clarify any concept they may still find confusing.

- A social studies teacher shows students a video about the Age of Enlightenment and instructs them to take notes. After watching the video, they find a partner and trade notes. Students add information to their own sets of notes if they notice an important idea they missed. Students then devise questions about the Age of Enlightenment and discuss them with another pair.

- After watching a video of several famous entrepreneurs, students in a personal finance class record the key themes mentioned by the entrepreneurs. Students partner and share their themes, noting similarities and differences in their conclusions. Pairs then either develop questions about entrepreneurship or brainstorm ideas for how they could become entrepreneurs.

### Differentiated Options

This section provides examples of ways you can modify this strategy for students who need additional support or opportunities to extend their learning.

- Allow students with reading or handwriting challenges to read their notes aloud with their partner.

- Encourage students who are ready for a further challenge to relate the content to previously learned class content or a real-world experience.

- Provide students who need academic support with a graphic organizer or a notetaking worksheet (such as the one in figure 3.6, page 42) to facilitate their notetaking.

## Strategy 11: Back to Back and Face to Face

*Back to Back and Face to Face* provides students time to think about a teacher's question before they discuss it with their partners. Teachers are sometimes dismayed by the awkward silence they receive in answer to a question or frustrated by how many of their students default to saying they don't have an answer. The amount of time students are given to provide an answer contributes to this pattern. Researchers Toyin Tofade, Jamie Elsner, and Stuart T. Haines (2013) note that increasing time for students to think about a question results in more and longer student responses and more follow-up questions. They also point out that fewer students answer "I don't know" when they're given more time to formulate an answer. This strategy ensures all students get the time they need to fully develop their thinking before sharing with a partner.

. . . . . . . . . . . . . . . . . . . . . . . . . . . . .

### CLASSROOM EXAMPLE

In mathematics class, the teacher projects two sets of data to summarize a lesson. Students stand back-to-back while viewing the data. Students independently decide which statistics would be appropriate to compare the center and spread of the two different data sets. The teacher instructs the pairs to face each other and share their thinking.

. . . . . . . . . . . . . . . . . . . . . . . . . . . . .

### Strategy Steps

Use the following steps to help you implement the *Back to Back and Face to Face* strategy.

1. Identify a reading, image, or data for students to analyze.

2. Create critical thinking questions for students to discuss.

3. Instruct students to find a partner and stand back-to-back.

4. Pose a question and allow students to independently think about the question. The more

challenging the question, the longer time students will need to formulate their answers.

5. Instruct students to turn around and face their partner and discuss the question.

6. Invite a few students to share their ideas with the class or pose another question. Repeat the process to answer additional questions.

### Variations

You can use the following variations in association with this strategy.

- Establish a protocol for which student speaks first (for example, the youngest partner or the one wearing warm or cool colors).

- Allow students to find a different partner after answering each question.

- Instruct students to raise their hands when they are ready to share. This lets the teacher know when students are ready to begin the discussion.

### Additional Content Area Examples

This section provides examples of ways you can connect this strategy to your teaching in different content areas.

- A language arts teacher instructs students to pair up and analyze the grammar issues in a piece of writing, identifying the most important changes that need to be made to improve the piece. Students receive time to think independently. After a few minutes, the teacher invites the students to face their partner and discuss their recommendations.

- A mathematics teacher pairs students and instructs them to stand back-to-back with a dry-erase board in their hands. The teacher reads and displays a problem. Students independently begin solving the problem using one of the problem-solving strategies they have learned (such as *look for a pattern*, *draw a picture*, or *make a table*). After a couple of minutes, students turn and face their partner and begin showing and explaining the strategy they chose, why they chose that strategy, and how they used it to solve the problem. The students discuss if there is a best strategy for solving the problem.

- A science teacher has students stand in pairs, back-to-back, and asks questions about energy waves and electromagnetic radiation. The students independently think about each question, then share responses with their partners. Once the pairs have discussed among themselves, they then share their responses with the class.

- After beginning their study of natural disasters, elementary students stand in pairs, back-to-back, as their social studies teacher reads aloud and projects the following questions for them to think about: "What's the worst storm you've ever been in? Where were you? What were you doing when the storm hit? Did the storm cause any damage? Describe your experience. What adaptations or changes did your family make after the storm?" After thinking independently, students turn around to share their ideas with their partners. Afterward, students share their ideas with the class.

- To introduce students to 20th century art after learning about earlier periods of art, a teacher shows students a 20th century painting. The teacher asks students how this painting shows traditional rules of art being broken to create new methods of art. Students stand in pairs, back-to-back, with a partner and consider the question, then turn to face their partner to discuss.

### Differentiated Options

This section provides examples of ways you can modify this strategy for students who need additional support or opportunities to extend their learning.

- Have students who are less confident about speaking prepare ideas ahead of time to share during their partner discussions.

- To support students who perform better with visuals, write or project the question on the board, allowing students to reference the question as they are thinking and discussing.

- To provide choices based on students' interests, post several questions and allow students to select the one they would like to answer.

- Invite students who need extended instruction to identify the best answer shared in a classroom discussion and provide reasoning to support their opinions.

## Discussion Questions

As you reflect on this chapter, consider the following five questions.

1.  In what ways do you currently utilize partner conversations in your classroom?

2.  Are partner conversations better for certain situations than assigning students to work in groups?

3.  How might the intended purpose for learning cause you to select different partner conversation strategies?

4.  Which partner strategy do you think you can use in your classroom?

5.  Which content area example gave you an idea for something you can do in your classroom?

## Action Steps

Use the following three activities to put this chapter's concepts to work in your own classroom.

1.  Provide the discussion stems from figure 3.1 (page 24) to students. Instruct them to use the stems to improve their use of academic language and focus their conversations. Reflect on the process. Did the discussion stems enhance the conversation? What would you change for future discussions?

2.  Select one of the strategies profiled in this chapter. How do you need to adapt it to meet the unique needs of the students in your classroom? Implement the strategy and reflect on ways to improve next time.

3.  Talk to another teacher about what strategies they use that involve peer discussions and student movement. Select one of their ideas to try in your classroom.

# CHAPTER 4

# Moving in Groups

*Mr. Rodriguez's language arts class is reading Harper Lee's* To Kill a Mockingbird. *He informs the class that they will visit several classroom stations to deepen their understanding of the book. Mr. Rodriguez organizes the students in groups and gives each a handout with tasks to complete at each station and space to take notes. Groups visit the following six stations.*

- ***Poetry analysis:*** *Groups read "I Know Why the Caged Bird Sings" by Maya Angelou. Students discuss how the poem is similar to and different from Lee's* To Kill a Mockingbird.

- ***Picture analysis:*** *Groups analyze different versions of the* To Kill a Mockingbird *cover, answer questions about how the cover images are similar and different, and draw inferences about why those images were used.*

- ***Life applications:*** *Groups define* courage *and discuss times when they demonstrated courage and failed to exhibit courage. Then, they discuss how their city is similar to and different from Maycomb, the novel's setting. Groups record their ideas on sticky notes and place them on two posters set up in the room. Students review the comments from other groups and discuss the varying perspectives.*

- ***Film applications:*** *Groups watch a segment from the film adaptation of* To Kill a Mockingbird *and compare how the film is similar to or different from the novel.*

- ***Conferencing station:*** *Groups bring their writing from the previous class to discuss. Students considered Atticus's statement that you never really understand a person "until you climb into his skin and walk around in it." They explore its meaning and how it relates to present day. The group discusses the quality of their writing including clear focus, logical sequence, details, and smooth transitions. Students make edits to their writing after discussion.*

- ***Review station:*** *Groups answer comprehension questions about the first few chapters of the novel.*

With this lesson, Mr. Rodriguez offers students a variety of ways to apply their knowledge and make new connections. This strategy creates high levels of student engagement as students work in groups to complete the six stations. Notice the role of the teacher, facilitating and supporting groups rather than lecturing or imparting information to students. Also notice that each station involves critical thinking activities. Students are tasked with analyzing and evaluating, which are high-level thinking skills.

While partner tasks, such as those outlined in chapter 3 (page 23), provide a high level of engagement for all students, group tasks (taken on by three or more members) build communication and cooperation. Many social and professional positions require students to function as a productive member of a group. Being able to collaborate with a variety of people toward a common goal is a valuable skill students need to transition into successful adult life (Stauffer, 2022).

In this chapter, I explore how students benefit from working in groups. I also share suggestions for assigning students to their groups and ensuring all students get equal airtime. The remainder of the chapter is devoted to thirteen strategies for integrating movement through student groups.

# Benefits of Working in Groups

When students work together in a group setting, they have an opportunity to build soft skills. As I noted in the introduction (page 1), teachers worldwide are expanding the skill sets they're fostering in students to include those key 21st century skills that enable workers to thrive in a rapidly evolving workforce. Allowing students to work in groups creates an environment where they develop and hone those skills, most notably learning skills (critical thinking, creativity, collaboration, communication) and life skills (flexibility, leadership, initiative, productivity, social skills; Stauffer, 2022).

As students collaborate in larger groups, they have opportunities to interact with a variety of peers and participate in building a classroom community. Given the many opinions raised in a group setting, students learn to compromise and problem solve—two important 21st century skills. Both pairs and groups provide students significantly more speaking time than is available when the teacher leads the discussion. As students work in their groups, teachers can fluidly move around the classroom providing formative feedback.

The strategies in this chapter place students in groups and allow them to learn together through movement. Group strategies provide all the benefits mentioned in the previous chapter and take learning to the next level by allowing students to build 21st century skills.

# Steps for Assigning Groups

Chapter 3 (page 23) suggests several methods of assigning partners. If you've been integrating partner discussions in your class, you've probably found methods of choosing partners that work best for your students. Now you can adapt those methods as needed to assign students to larger groups. Consider the following creative ways to group students.

- Place stickers on index cards and provide a card to each student. Students with matching stickers form a group.

- Pull matching UNO cards from a deck that represent the number of groups you want and ensure you have enough cards for each student in the group. Provide each student with a UNO card and instruct them to form groups by matching their cards together.

- Buy or create puzzles with the number of pieces corresponding to the number of members you designate for each group. Provide a puzzle piece to each student and instruct them to collaborate to complete their puzzles. The students who have the matching puzzle pieces form a group.

Other grouping strategies could support differentiation.

- Create a list of group roles. Then instruct students to choose a role they wish to fill and create groups so that each group contains a student performing each role.

- Organize students into groups that represent their diverse abilities. This is a great way to model how students' unique strengths and needs can complement each other.

- Create groups that represent student ability and offer differentiated versions of the assignment to meet the group's readiness level.

As groups are larger than pairs, teachers may need to monitor so all group members participate equally. Giving each group member talking chips—tokens such as playing cards, poker chips, or markers that a student spends in exchange for a turn to talk—is a way to ensure that all students participate equally in the conversations. When a student uses up all their chips, the student waits until all the other students have spent their chips to speak again. This ensures a balanced group discussion and reinforces flexibility, initiative, leadership, and social skills.

Another way to monitor equal airtime is to assign roles within the team, including a notetaker, timekeeper, and facilitator, to increase student participation and reduce the likelihood that one student will dominate the discussion, opt out of responsibility, or take on too many roles within the group.

In the previous chapter, I provided discussion stems, discussion preparation suggestions, and question stems to be used for pairing strategies. (See Steps to Prepare for Discussion, page 25 in chapter 3.) You can adapt the same tools for group strategies as well.

## Strategy 12: Carousel Questioning

*Carousel Questioning* challenges students to move while accessing critical thinking. Using this strategy, students work together on questions posted around the room on large chart paper. Each group receives a set amount of time to work on each question before being asked to switch. They then rotate to the next question with their group. Teachers can carefully construct questions that require critical thinking, while students can enjoy moving around the room providing answers.

. . . . . . . . . . . . . . . . . . . . . . . . . . . . . .

### CLASSROOM EXAMPLE

After a fractions lesson, the mathematics teacher forms groups to investigate real-world problems and tasks students with equitably dividing candy, pizza, and other food items. The teacher posts food problems around the room on chart paper. Each group selects the problem they want to work on first. After completing the problem and agreeing on the answer, groups rotate to the next problem in a circular pattern around the room.

. . . . . . . . . . . . . . . . . . . . . . . . . . . . . .

### Strategy Steps

Use the following steps to help you implement the *Carousel Questioning* strategy.

1.  Prepare a series of questions for students to discuss based on a recent lesson.

2.  Post the questions on chart paper spaced out along the classroom walls.

3.  Create small groups of three to five students, depending on the number of questions. There should be at least as many questions as there are groups.

4.  Provide each group with a unique color of marker to write their answers on the chart paper. This helps the teacher identify each group's contribution. Students review their questions and discuss their answers. Groups rotate the scribe role so that, for each question, a different person is the scribe.

5.  After around two minutes, depending on the complexity of the question, instruct students to rotate to the right to the next prompt and add new information to the chart paper or expand on the information that is already posted.

6.  When students arrive back at their original chart paper, instruct groups to work together to write a two-sentence summary of the information on their paper to share with the class.

### Variations

You can use the following variations in association with this strategy.

*   If the classroom does not allow much space for movement, post the discussion questions in the hallway or another larger area. Students often enjoy learning in different locations.

*   Allow students to record their thoughts on a graphic organizer before joining their group.

*   Sometimes students are reluctant to add more thoughts when they first see others' ideas. In this case, allow students to write responses on sticky notes and cover them with a second sheet of chart paper. Subsequent groups record their thinking before lifting the sheet to view the ideas left by previous groups.

*   Hide discussion questions outside on the playground or another area for students to first find the questions and then record their answers on their own paper.

*   Designate a scribe for each group.

*   Allow students to draw pictures instead of writing sentences.

*   Assign students to use technology (such as Loom or Screencastify) to build Google Slides with voiceovers. Encourage each student to sign up to complete a task such as writing the text, adding images, or creating voiceovers.

### Additional Content Area Examples

This section provides examples of ways you can connect this strategy to your teaching in different content areas.

*   A language arts teacher posts chart paper around the room, displaying discussion questions about effective speaking skills including qualities of

effectively written speeches, successful presentation skills, and common mistakes public speakers make. Students are split into groups and assigned one of the chart papers. Each group answers the question posed on the chart paper. Then the teacher instructs each group to move clockwise to the next question. This process repeats until every group has answered each question.

- A mathematics teacher displays poster paper containing the names of geometric transformations (translations, rotations, reflections, and dilations). Groups choose one transformation and write and draw as much information about it as they can. When finished, the groups move to the next poster, adding more information with sticky notes. When the students return to their original poster, they summarize the most important ideas and share them with the class.

- A science teacher posts chart paper around the room identifying different types of energy. Groups move to their first teacher-assigned station, where the students begin defining, drawing pictures, and giving examples of each type of energy for five minutes. Once the timer goes off, students rotate to the next station, where they begin adding ideas about the next type of energy.

- After conducting a lesson on civic and political institutions, a social studies teacher posts pieces of chart paper around the room that list various systems of government, including monarchy, democracy, republic, and theocracy. Students are placed in groups that rotate around the room to each paper. Each group discusses the term's definition, an example, and a symbolic picture. Then, they individually record in their graphic organizer their definition, example, and symbol. Groups rotate to the next piece of chart paper when the timer signals.

- An art teacher posts chart paper around the room containing different styles of portraits. Working in groups, students observe a portrait and identify the style. Students individually record their thinking on a graphic organizer. After a five-minute timer signal, the students move to the next portrait.

### Differentiated Options

This section provides examples of ways you can modify this strategy for students who need additional support or opportunities to extend their learning.

- Allow students who need more time to move at their own pace. Give select students modified learning objectives that require them to complete fewer questions on their graphic organizer.

- Provide an additional challenge station and question for students who finish early.

- Allow English learners to work with peers who speak the same home language. This allows them to make connections in their most familiar language as well as in English and build academic vocabulary.

- Instruct students who would benefit from extension activities to compose high-level questions to contribute to whole-class discussion.

## Strategy 13: Rotation Stations

In *Rotation Stations*, student groups move around the room to various stations where they interact with different concepts. Teachers interact with each group as needed to facilitate the learning process. Stations can be tailored toward different learning preferences, including the use of media, creative learning opportunities, and real-world applications. This helps teachers address students' diverse interests. To help students with this strategy, provide a notetaking guide like the one in figure 4.1.

### CLASSROOM EXAMPLE

The science teacher places students in small groups to learn about animal adaptation and provides a handout for taking notes as they visit different stations. One station has a video about how genetic variation affects animal survival. After watching the short video, the group discusses the questions on the notetaking guide and records their answers. At another station, students analyze pictures of fossils to identify differences between these animals and current animal species. At a third station, students read about natural selection and adaptations and complete comprehension questions on their notetaking guide. At a fourth station, students analyze a picture of an animal in their community and hypothesize how the animal has adapted to survive.

| Notetaking Guide | |
|---|---|
| **Instructions:** Write the name of each station you visit in the first column. Record your notes in the second column. | |
| **Station 1: Genetic variation video** | Which type of selection tends to increase genetic variation? *Disruptive selection increases genetic variation. With this, extreme phenotypes are favored over intermediate ones, which causes the formation of new species.* What are two main sources of genetic variation? *Random mutations and genetic recombination. Mutations are changes in DNA coding that change an organism's physiology, behavior, or appearance. Recombination, or the mixing of genetic material, produces variation during the process of crossing over, which happens in meiosis.* Why is genetic variation important? *Without genetic variation, organisms can't evolve or adapt. Genetic variation promotes natural selection, increasing an organism's ability to survive.* |
| **Station 2: Differences in the fossil record** | Fossil 1: *A spider fossil; looks almost exactly like a spider today* Fossil 2: *Looks like an ancient eel-like fish with teeth; teeth look more like a shark today* Fossil 3: *Looks like an early elephant with large teeth, but current elephant is taller* |
| **Station 3: Natural selection and adaptations** | Define natural selection in your own words. *Natural selection is the process where organisms adapt to their environment to help them survive and produce offspring.* Define adaptation. *Adaptation is where an organism or species changes to better survive in their environment.* Name a way you have adapted at school. *I wear a jacket in your class because you always have the air conditioner turned up.* |
| **Station 4: Adaptation and survival** | *Elk have adapted to survive in our harsh winters in the mountains. They have thick, smooth fur that keeps them warm. Male elk grow new horns each year, which helps them attract females and fight elk battles.* |

**Figure 4.1:** Sample notetaking guide.

*Visit* **go.SolutionTree.com/studentengagement** *for a free reproducible version of this figure.*

## Strategy Steps

Use the following steps to help you implement the *Rotation Stations* strategy.

1. Decide on the topic to use for this strategy.

2. Create stations that address different aspects of the topic. Consider how you will use media, real-world applications, high-level questions, and creative learning options. Be sure to appeal to your students' various interests as you're incorporating high-level tasks.

3. Divide students into groups and provide note-taking guides for them to record their work at each station. While groups discuss the answers, each student should record answers on their notetaking guide.

4. Assign each group a station to begin their rotation. Either allow students to move to the next station at their own pace or set a timer to indicate when groups should rotate.

5. When the timer goes off, instruct students to move to the next station. Repeat until all groups have completed each station.

### Variations

You can use the following variations in association with this strategy.

- Have one station be the teacher leading a discussion or an activity to help students reinforce key concepts and address misconceptions.

- Locate the stations outside the classroom—perhaps in the library or gym so that students may access resources available in those locations.

### Additional Content Area Examples

This section provides examples of ways you can connect this strategy to your teaching in different content areas.

- During a unit about Ray Bradbury's *Fahrenheit 451*, a language arts teacher instructs students to rotate through stations covering vocabulary, plot, characterization, and themes found in the novel. Students divide into groups and begin working at their assigned station. Each group rotates through the stations until they've completed the full circuit.

- To review laws of exponents, a mathematics teacher creates different stations with example problems to solve for each law of exponents. The stations include multiplying powers (same base), dividing powers, power of a power, multiplying powers (same exponent), negative exponents, and powers with exponent zero. As students rotate to each station, they write the rule on their notetaking guide and then solve the problems using the rule. When finished solving, the students then check their answers with the answer key posted at the front of the room. When the time runs out, the teacher cues students to rotate to the next station.

- A science teacher sets up stations around the room where students will learn about the growth, development, and reproduction of different organisms. Each station includes either a video, reading passage, pictures, or infographic. After viewing the informational source, students work with their group to answer two analytical questions in their notes. The teacher allows groups to rotate through the stations at their own speed, redirecting students as needed to avoid overcrowding.

- During a macroeconomics unit, a teacher sets up stations where students will learn about how taxes are collected by the government and used to provide different goods and services to society. Students rotate between three different stations to watch a video that explains the purpose of taxes and how they are collected, play a computer game that simulates a market economy, and read a short story and answer questions about the role that taxes have on goods and services. After they complete the activity in each station, they answer a few questions on their notetaking guide and discuss their ideas with their group.

- A music teacher designs a series of stations where students can learn about the instruments of the orchestra. At one station, students play instrument bingo by listening to recordings of various instruments playing a short solo and identifying the instruments on a bingo card. At the next station, students classify instrument cards into the four families of instruments as quickly and accurately as possible and then check their work against the answer key. Next, students explore a website to learn about the unique qualities of woodwind and brass instruments while answering questions on their notetaking guide. At another station, students learn about string and percussion instruments by composing a unique rhythm. At the final station, students watch a video of a conductor leading various patterns; afterward, students practice conducting those patterns together as a small group.

### Differentiated Options

This section provides examples of ways you can modify this strategy for students who need additional support or opportunities to extend their learning.

- Present the material in various formats (for example, audio, visual) to allow students to access the knowledge in different ways.

- Assign each student a role based on their talents. For example, one student reads the station directions to the group, another keeps the group on task, and a third asks questions about key information for clarification. These roles focus group members on the task while allowing students to contribute their skills to the group.

- Have students who need additional support rotate to a teacher-led station where they can work on vocabulary terms or other concepts that require scaffolding.

- Provide a challenge station where highly proficient students can use the learning to solve a real-world problem.

- Provide readings on audio using sources such as Librivox, YouTube, or other public domain audiobooks. Use resources such as Common Lit or Newsela to provide readings at varying Lexile levels when possible.

## Strategy 14: Debate Team Carousel

Identifying various viewpoints is a high-level thinking task, one that is embedded into the *Debate Team Carousel* strategy. Students exchange papers with peers to gather additional information and various perspectives. To help students with this strategy, provide them with a graphic organizer like the one in figure 4.2.

. . . . . . . . . . . . . . . . . . . . . . . . . . . . . . . .

### CLASSROOM EXAMPLE

In a science class, students consider, based on their readings, whether climate change is largely human-caused. Using a graphic organizer, each student records their perspective on the issue and cites evidence to support their claims. In groups of three, students then pass their paper to another group member, and that group member writes a supporting argument based on evidence in the articles. Students pass their paper again, and a third student describes an opposing argument. Finally, the paper returns to the original student. The student considers the diverse perspectives group members provided and writes a conclusion on the controversial issue in the last box.

. . . . . . . . . . . . . . . . . . . . . . . . . . . . . . . .

| Graphic Organizer |
|---|
| **I think:** |
| *I agree with the Myths article that stated that the rapid warming now can't be explained by natural cycles of warming and cooling. These changes would normally occur over hundreds of thousands of years. Now they are happening much faster.* |
| **A supporting argument:** |
| *The Environmental Protection Agency, a reputable source, stated that human activities have caused large amounts of carbon dioxide and other greenhouse gases to be released into the atmosphere. This process has affected the earth's climate. While natural processes like changes in the sun's energy and volcanic eruptions impact the earth's climate, it is extremely likely that human activities are the major cause of warming.* |
| **An opposing argument:** |
| *According to the Perspective article, climate varies naturally over a wide range of time scales. Changes in the earth's orbit and rotation, variations in solar activity, volcanic activity, and changes in naturally occurring carbon dioxide concentrations are causing climate changes.* |
| **In conclusion, I think:** |
| *Global warming is primarily human caused. While temperature does fluctuate naturally, it is changing faster now due to human actions. Greenhouse gases and carbon dioxide that are being released into our atmosphere are negatively impacting Earth's climate.* |

**Figure 4.2:** Debate team carousel graphic organizer.

*Visit* **go.SolutionTree.com/studentengagement** *for a free reproducible version of this figure.*

### Strategy Steps

Use the following steps to help you implement the *Debate Team Carousel* strategy.

1. Select a topic that can be viewed from at least two different perspectives.

2. Distribute a graphic organizer (see figure 4.2) with four boxes where students: (1) record their opinion, (2) add a supporting argument, (3) add an opposing argument, and (4) record a conclusion drawn from their classmates' writing.

3. Create groups of three students and instruct them to sit together in a circle.

4. Instruct students to complete the first box by recording their opinion about the topic.

5. Ask students to pass the paper to the right and the next student adds a supporting argument.

6. Ask students to pass the paper to the right again, and the next person identifies an opposing argument.

7. When the paper returns to the original person, have the student record a concluding opinion based on the others group members' statements.

### Variations

You can use the following variations in association with this strategy.

- Allow students to use digital tools like Padlet, Jamboard, or Flip to record their answers and respond to each other by posting digital sticky notes or response videos. The final post should capture all the viewpoints mentioned and include evidence to support their opinion.

- Use *Musical Debate* (Kruse, n.d.), a similar strategy in which the teacher poses the prompt that can be debated and then plays music for students to move around the classroom and think about the prompt while noting their thoughts. Students then find two partners near them and form a group. In the trios, the students select a role: pro, con, and neutral. The pro role shares first for one minute, and then the con role for one minute. Finally, the neutral role summarizes, adds on any points, and identifies any logical fallacies. Students record thoughts as

their peers present and participate in a rebuttal round to respond to the arguments and thoughts posed by others (Kruse, n.d.).

### Additional Content Area Examples

This section provides examples of ways you can connect this strategy to your teaching in different content areas.

- In a discussion about George Orwell's *1984*, a language arts teacher poses the following question: "Is reality subjective, or does an objective reality exist outside of personal perception?" The teacher then distributes a graphic organizer. In the first box, students record their opinion; in the second box, students provide evidence and reasoning for their arguments; in the third box, students address rebuttals; and in the fourth box, students provide their opinions on what others answered.

- A mathematics teacher displays a data graphic about COVID-19. In groups, students analyze the data and draw conclusions about the information. They write a newspaper article heading that the graphic could be used for. They then pass their paper to the right, and students take turns adding a snippet they believe would have been found in that article. Next, students pass their paper again, recording inaccurate conclusions. Finally, the first person gets the paper back and writes their opinion about what others recorded.

- A science teacher asks students to identify causes and effects of global warming. Students form groups of three and work independently to record their responses on a graphic organizer. Students pass their papers to the person beside them who writes a supporting argument to the original student's claim. This student passes the paper to the person beside them, who writes an opposing claim. The paper is then returned to its original owner who will then write a conclusion based on their peers' statements.

- A geography teacher asks students to select their favorite climate region and describe why they would like to live there. Students record their opinions on their graphic organizers, then pass their papers to the right. The next student fills in the supporting details of the argument and passes the paper to the right again. The next group member records an opposing argument. That student passes the paper to the original group member, who writes a concluding statement in response to the group's work.

- A physical education teacher poses the question: "Should all students be required to take a physical education course each year of high school?" Students record their initial thinking in the graphic organizer. A group member then adds additional support to the argument. The third partner adds an opposing viewpoint. Students consider all the evidence noted and create their own final argument.

### Differentiated Options

This section provides examples of ways you can modify this strategy for students who need additional support or opportunities to extend their learning.

- Scaffold the reading in advance or in a prior lesson for students who struggle with reading comprehension so they can better understand the article. Consider allowing the student to read one section of the article at the time and make notes in the margin or discuss it with a partner.

- For students who are ready for higher levels of challenge, allow them to extend the lesson by finding additional research articles that support their final opinion.

## Strategy 15: Tableau

*Tableau* (Teacher Toolkit, 2021) allows students to represent what they are learning by acting out a scene. This strategy provides students an opportunity to move their bodies to demonstrate their understanding. During this activity, students can move beyond summarizing information to higher-level thinking tasks by identifying the most important scene in a book, most important leader in a history movement, worst mistake in a historical conflict, key lines in a poem, or other subject-specific task.

Students in a social studies class have been learning about different historical events and historical figures. After covering the significance of each U.S. Civil War event, the teacher tasks students with reenacting one turning point event by depicting a scene in which they play a historical figure. Afterward, each group shares its rationale for why this event was the most important event in the war.

### Strategy Steps

Use the following steps to help you implement the *Tableau* strategy.

1. Form groups of three to five students.
2. Have students identify a topic or area to display. Each group should then plan a way to act it out.
3. Provide students time to practice their tableau.
4. Have groups present the tableau they created.
5. Instruct each group to justify their selection of this topic or area to the class.

### Variations

You can use the following variations in association with this strategy.

- Provide groups with their topic, but instruct them to keep it a secret so when they act it out, the remainder of the class can guess the event or person represented.

- Select a student to make a short statement about the tableau they created or the role they are playing once they are all in place for the presentation.

- Ask groups to incorporate one mistake into their presentation; classmates try to guess the mistake at the end.

### Additional Content Area Examples

This section provides examples of ways you can connect this strategy to your teaching in different content areas.

- After writing their own stories in groups, students select the best part of the story and then create a tableau of the scene and perform it for the class.

- To review parent functions, a mathematics teacher assigns students to create a tableau by using their arms to pose as the graphs of those parent functions. Groups present their tableau, and their classmates must guess which parent function they enacted.

- After introducing Newton's laws of motion, a science teacher divides students into groups and instructs them to choose one of the three laws to act out. They act out how forces interact with different objects. Students then present their chosen law to the rest of the class.

- After completing an economics unit, a social studies teacher asks students to select the most important word from the unit, such as *producer, consumer, product, labor, supply,* or *demand.* Students discuss their selected term and decide how they will demonstrate it to the class. Groups perform their tableau for the class. The class tries to guess the word they are demonstrating.

- A family and consumer science teacher assigns students to reenact learning about kitchen safety by creating a tableau of how to correctly use various kitchen tools and appliances. Each group must include one mistake in their presentation. Students rehearse and perform their tableau for the class. Classmates try to guess the mistake.

### Differentiated Options

This section provides examples of ways you can modify this strategy for students who need additional support or opportunities to extend their learning.

- Offer students who have difficulty writing the option to use the voice-dictation tools (included in Google Docs, for example) instead of writing their script or designate a scribe for their group.

- For students who need additional structure, provide a handout that details instructions for creating a tableau. The handout can cue students to brainstorm ideas, select the best idea, develop ways to structure their tableau, and mark off tasks as they're completed.

## Strategy 16: Yes and No Chart

The *Yes and No Chart* strategy helps students reflect on their own learning. Researchers Xiaoyu Jia, Weijian Li, and Liren Cao (2019) note that students' ability to think about their thinking, metacognition, is a critical component of creativity. As students think about their own cognitive processes, they can identify understandings that are clear or confusing. The activity can also serve as a formative assessment, which the teacher can use to inform further instruction.

### CLASSROOM EXAMPLE

Students in a language arts class learn about the structure and format of a research paper and how to evaluate a research paper using a rubric. After the lesson, students use a Yes and No chart, indicating topics and skills they understood in the *Yes* column and those that are still unclear in the *No* column. The teacher uses this information as a formative assessment and designs further instruction to address the topics mentioned in the *No* column.

### Strategy Steps

Use the following steps to help you implement the *Yes and No Chart* strategy.

1. Create groups of three to five students.

2. Post chart paper at different stations around the room. Divide the paper into *Yes* and *No* columns.

3. Instruct groups to go to one of the pieces of chart paper and list topics they understand completely in the *Yes* column and list items that are unclear and need more explanation in the *No* column.

4. Merge two groups together. Each group provides information about the items listed in their *No* column. This process repeats until the groups have discussed all the unknown items on each list.

5. Facilitate a classroom discussion, inviting each group to share any remaining items in their *No* column and talk about them as a class to answer questions and clear up misunderstandings.

### Variations

You can use the following variations in association with this strategy.

- When a group shares their *No* items, have students in other groups move toward the group or raise their hand if they have a similar item on their list.

- Instruct students to list their *Yes* and *No* items on a digital board like Padlet or Jamboard.

- Instead of starting in a group, have students work individually to record statements they learned and questions they still have about the topic. Students can then work in groups to discuss them or compile them on the chart paper.

- When studying a concept, have students record examples of the concept in the *Yes* column and non-examples in the *No* column.

- When groups finish writing on their chart paper, ask them to rotate to another group and address one of the topics in the *No* column by leaving a sticky note with information. Groups then rotate around the room to address at least one of the *No* items on each group's chart.

### Additional Content Area Examples

This section provides examples of ways you can connect this strategy to your teaching in different content areas.

- After learning about the concepts of theme and central idea, a language arts teacher places students into groups. In their groups, students create a chart featuring a *Yes* and a *No* column. Students record topics they understood about the lesson under the *Yes* column and topics they did not fully grasp in the *No* column.

- A mathematics teacher gives students ratio problems on cut-out pieces of paper. In groups, students work to solve the problems. When they are confident they know the concept presented in the problem, they tape it to the *Yes* column. If they are less confident in their answer or can't figure out the answer, they tape it to the *No* column. Two groups merge and explain the problems and any misconceptions that arise with the problems in the *No* column.

- After teaching about natural selection and the adaptations that populations develop in response to it, a science teacher places students into groups and instructs them to record topics they understood from the lesson in the *Yes* column of their chart and list ideas they didn't fully understand in the *No* column. Once they are finished writing, groups merge and work together to clear up the items in their *No* columns.

- After teaching about domestic and foreign policy, a social studies teacher assigns students to groups and instructs them to create a Yes and No chart. The students record policies they understand and feel confident about in the *Yes* column and policies or concepts they don't understand as well in the *No* column. Once each group creates its chart, the group merges with another group and shares charts, clarifying anything written in the other group's *No* column.

- After teaching about the elements of art (for example, color, line, shape, form, and texture), groups record topics and skills they understand in the *Yes* column and those they don't in the *No* column. Groups share their chart with another group to clarify misunderstandings.

### Differentiated Options

This section provides examples of ways you can modify this strategy for students who need additional support or opportunities to extend their learning.

- Display topics and ask students to use color-coded stickers to label what they understand (green for *Yes*) and what they do not understand (red for *No*). This option involves less writing for students who struggle with their handwriting.

- Facilitate a class discussion and encourage students to volunteer to explain any topics in the *No* column as they may have a new approach to explaining the topic.

## Strategy 17: Conver-Stations

*Conver-Stations* allows students to participate in small-group discussions with a rotation of peers. It is an energizing strategy that offers many opportunities for movement. With thoughtful design, the questions in this activity can engage students in high-level thinking.

## CLASSROOM EXAMPLE

At the beginning of a reading class, the teacher distributes a copy of the poem "Rock 'N' Roll Band" by Shel Silverstein to students and reads it aloud. The teacher has set up various stations where groups of students can analyze different elements of the poem. At station one, students discuss comprehension questions about the poem. Station two has students discuss the advantages and disadvantages of being in a band. A third station has students examine the poet's choice of words. At the fourth station, students examine the voice and tone of the poem. The final station challenges students to examine the poem's structure. In groups of four, students review the materials at each station and discuss the questions. Then, groups number off from one to four to form new groups. Threes and fours remain with the original source, while ones move to another group where another number one left, and twos move to another group where a number two left. Groups again review the source and discuss.

### Strategy Steps

Use the following steps to help you implement the *Conver-Stations* strategy.

1. Design enough stations so that each group of four will have different materials or questions. Each station should have discussion questions based on a reading, video, audio clip, or photo.

2. Create groups of four and have students number off from one to four in the groups.

3. Remind students of group norms: using sentence stems during group discussion, ensuring equitable participation in the group, and staying on topic.

4. Provide time for each group to review the source and engage in discussion based on the questions for two to five minutes.

5. Instruct all students who are a one or two to move to another group while threes and fours remain in the original group. As students stand up and move, they should hold up their numbers on their fingers in the air, find another student with that same number, and switch spots. The students who were in the group previously share their prompt and thoughts and ask the new members their thoughts for two to three minutes.

6. After finishing the discussion, instruct students who are numbers three and four to move to another station and repeat the process. Students should always move to a station they haven't visited yet. Repeat the process until students have visited all the stations.

### Variations

You can use the following variations in association with this strategy.

- Have all students rotate through each station together, changing jobs or roles in each station.

- Ask each group to leave behind their thoughts in a box or envelope. Once the new group reviews the sources and forms their own thoughts, they open the box or envelope and read the other groups' thoughts, noting similar or different ideas.

### Additional Content Area Examples

This section provides examples of ways you can connect this strategy to your teaching in different content areas.

- To discuss the rhetoric in Truman Capote's novel *In Cold Blood*, a language arts teacher creates four stations, each featuring a document. Documents one and two have sections from the novel; document three includes mug shots and crime scene photos; and document four is a news article from 1959 about the murders. Students split into groups of four, then number themselves one through four. Students examine the document at their station and then answer questions about rhetoric based on the document. For document one, students look for techniques used in Capote's writing; for document two, students highlight ethical appeals (ethos) used in Capote's writing; in document three, students record emotional appeals (pathos) in the photos; and in document four, students record logical appeals (logos) in the news article. After students complete the station they are in with their groups, two of the students stay where they are and share their group's ideas, while the other two move to a different group to hear new ideas from other students at different stations.

- A mathematics teacher assigns groups of four an image of a large number of objects and instructs them to estimate the number of objects in the image. Students discuss their estimates and their strategies for determining them. After some time, two students move to a different group, see their image, and hear ideas from the original group members. The students new to the group add any other ideas, observations, or strategies they may have.

- After teaching about Earth's systems, a science teacher sets up four different stations focused on the hydrosphere, atmosphere, geosphere, and biosphere. In groups of four, students at each station watch a video, then answer several discussion questions about information they learned in the video. Once each group has completed its station's tasks, two students switch stations to learn about another station.

- A social studies teacher passes out a copy of the Magna Carta to each student, and students read this document in groups of four. Students then complete questions with their group members at each of four stations. At one station, students highlight three sentences they feel are the most important and explain why. In another, students analyze the document and write down any questions they have. The remaining two stations help students further analyze the document and consider its purpose. After students complete one station, two students stay where they are and share their group's ideas, and two move to a different station to hear new ideas from other students.

- The teacher of a business course divides students into groups and sets up four stations about the four main types of entrepreneurs: (1) small businesses, (2) scalable startups, (3) large companies, and (4) social entrepreneurs. Each station has readings, materials, or videos with discussion questions where students can brainstorm advantages, challenges, and examples of each type.

After students complete one station, two students from each group move to a different group to learn about other types of entrepreneurs.

### Differentiated Options

This section provides examples of ways you can modify this strategy for students who need additional support or opportunities to extend their learning.

- Assign students roles and jobs to clarify expectations.
- Provide reading materials in audio format.
- Supply closed captioning translations for videos and audio.
- Allow students to listen to pre-recorded directions at each station.

## Strategy 18: Fishbowl

*Fishbowl* creates the opportunity for student-led discussion about key unit ideas. This activity boosts engagement because students take ownership of their learning. Students prepare by answering critical thinking questions prior to the discussion. This activity integrates movement by shifting students in and out of the circle of discussion.

### CLASSROOM EXAMPLE

After reading *The Lord of the Flies* as a class, the language arts teacher prepares discussion questions. The class divides into two groups, with half of the students sitting at desks in an inner circle and the rest sitting in the outer circle. Students in the inner circle discuss key details from the novel. When a student from the outside circle wants to join in the discussion, they walk to a person in the inner circle who is not speaking and tap their desk to switch places. This continues until all the questions have been answered.

### Strategy Steps

Use the following steps to help you implement the *Fishbowl* strategy.

1. Instruct students to read and answer a list of critical thinking questions you've prepared ahead of time. Encourage students to prepare thoughtful questions for discussion.

2. Move student desks into two concentric circles with a small circle of desks in the center of the room and a larger circle outside of the small circle.

3. Initiate the discussion with a question and encourage students from the inner circle to respond while the students on the outside of the circle listen as audience members. When a student from the audience is ready to join the discussion, they tap the desk of a person in the inner circle who is not speaking and then switch positions.

4. Continue the student-led, teacher-guided discussion until all the questions have been answered.

### Variations

You can use the following variations in association with this strategy.

- Have students in the audience take notes, listing the most important point made and any ideas they disagree with.

- Use this strategy before a lesson or unit to ignite student thinking about the content that will be covered.

- Instead of using tapping to allow students to join the conversation, have the outside and inside circles switch places at certain points of the discussion.

- Distribute two cards to each student. Require all students to pose questions or provide comments during the discussion. Each time they participate, students raise a card for you to collect. When students have used both of their cards, they must wait until all the other students in the circle have used up their cards before they can participate again, to ensure all students contribute equally.

- Try *Socratic Soccer Ball*, in which you instruct students to form a circle after reading a selection or learning about a topic. Ask students to pass around a ball as you play music for a few seconds. Once you turn the music off, pose a question to the student holding the ball.

### Additional Content Area Examples

This section provides examples of ways you can connect this strategy to your teaching in different content areas.

- To discuss ideas such as masculinity, ambition, and guilt in William Shakespeare's *Macbeth*, a language arts teacher tasks students with developing a list of five thought-provoking discussion questions. Students form two circles, one within the other. The inner circle of students poses and responds to questions while the outer circle of students listens and prepares to join the conversation. After ten minutes, the teacher instructs the students in the outer circle to switch places with the students in the inner circle, then discussion within the inner circle resumes.

- A mathematics teacher arranges the classroom for a fishbowl discussion on a novel the class has been reading: *Flatland: A Romance of Many Dimensions* by Edwin A. Abbott. Students in the inner circle discuss the questions the teacher prepared about the mathematics in the novel, while those in the outer circle take notes. Students then switch circles and answer more discussion questions.

- After teaching about seeds spreading throughout the world, a science teacher provides students with participation cards and instructs them to form two circles for a fishbowl discussion. Students move to the outer circle when they have spent their cards by participating twice in the discussion. Then, a student from the outer circle who hasn't participated joins the inner circle.

- After teaching about the movement of people, ideas, and goods to and within North America, a social studies teacher creates questions that prompt students to consider the cultural, economic, and environmental factors that encouraged this migration. The teacher arranges students into two fishbowl circles, and students in the inner circle answer questions while students in the outer circle listen. Students in the outer circle switch places with a student in the inner circle when they want to share an idea.

- A teacher of family consumer science creates a list of questions about how drugs and alcohol affect the body. Students stand in a circle and pass a ball until the music stops. At that point, the student holding the ball answers a question posed by the teacher.

### Differentiated Options

This section provides examples of ways you can modify this strategy for students who need additional support or opportunities to extend their learning.

- Allow students who need extra time to prepare statements and questions about the topic before the discussion.

- Designate students who need more movement as the scribes of the discussion. Scribes take notes about what is being said while moving around the classroom.

## Strategy 19: Small-Group Scoot

*Small-Group Scoot* encourages students to move while answering questions, activating the body and the mind. Students answer questions or complete tasks while standing at their desks in small groups. After they complete the task, students rotate (scoot) to the next desk to complete the next task. At the conclusion of the activity, students view peers' diverse perspectives and discuss misunderstandings or misconceptions.

• • • • • • • • • • • • • • • • • • • • • • • • • • •

### CLASSROOM EXAMPLE

After learning about geometric shapes, a mathematics teacher distributes question cards to each group of students. Each student takes a question card and places it on their desk. The students stand up and complete the task, recording their answers on their paper. The teacher says "Scoot" and students rotate clockwise to the next desk and work on the next task.

• • • • • • • • • • • • • • • • • • • • • • • • • • •

### Strategy Steps

Use the following steps to help you implement the *Small-Group Scoot* strategy.

1. Create a set of questions or tasks for each group, and have the group arrange their desks together.

2. Distribute one question or task to each desk with a blank piece of paper for students to record their answers.

3. Instruct groups to take turns rotating to each desk. They should answer the question or complete the task on the desk and write their answers on paper. Students fold under their response so the next group does not see it.

4. After allowing time for students to complete the task or question, say "Scoot" to cue groups to move in a clockwise direction to the next task or question.

5. Instruct groups to unfold the answers sheet to reveal all the answers and allow time for them to discuss the different answers to each question along with any misunderstandings.

### Variations

You can use the following variations in association with this strategy.

- Have students scoot to the next station at their own pace rather than within a time limit.

- Instruct students to use different colored pencils or pens so it is clear who recorded each response to each question. As groups discuss, they can recognize whose answer was different or unique.

### Additional Content Area Examples

This section provides examples of ways you can connect this strategy to your teaching in different content areas.

- While reading Chinua Achebe's novel *Things Fall Apart*, a language arts teacher prepares questions about Achebe's craft and perspective. The teacher arranges the desks into groups of four, placing one question at each desk. Questions may pertain to excerpts from the novel as well as from Achebe's other writings, such as "English and the African Writer." Students stand behind a desk and answer the question at their desks. Then, they fold their answer and scoot to the next desk.

- A mathematics teacher gives students a paper with a linear equation at the top and a coordinate grid. The students graph their given equation and then fold the paper down so that others cannot see the original equation. Students move to the next desk, where they write the linear equation based on the graph the previous student drew. They then fold the paper down so that the next student does not see the graph. This continues until all students have graphed and written a couple of equations. Then, students open the papers and determine if the graph at the bottom matches the equation at the top. If not, students should work together to find where the error occurred.

- After teaching about how humans affect the land, vegetation, streams, oceans, and air, a science teacher gives students task cards and breaks them into groups. The teacher instructs them to think of examples, explain ideas, evaluate different human impacts, and brainstorm solutions to environmental issues. Students fold their answers and scoot to answer the next questions.

- A social studies teacher creates a series of questions regarding the roles and responsibilities of subjects in empires between AD 600 to AD 1600 as compared to those of citizens in modern countries. Students respond and record their answers, then scoot to the next question.

- After reading about credit, debt, and money management, the teacher of a business class distributes various case studies to different stations around the room and tasks groups with assuming the role of a financial counselor recommending solutions to their client. Each group reads the case study and responds to the questions. Once they've finished, they fold down their ideas and rotate to the next station, repeating the process until all groups have visited each station.

### Differentiated Options

This section provides examples of ways you can modify this strategy for students who need additional support or opportunities to extend their learning.

- To extend the learning, create a different set of questions or tasks for high-level groups.

- Allow students who need additional support to have a designated partner within the group or to carry out a predetermined role to ensure they are able to participate in the group task.

## Strategy 20: Walkabout

Just as major corporate leaders have walking meetings, students benefit from walking discussions.

The *Walkabout* strategy increases blood circulation and helps students refocus as they discuss content. Teachers can design high-level questions that interest students to form the basis for the discussion.

### CLASSROOM EXAMPLE

To prepare to read about examples of discrimination, a social studies teacher groups students and instructs them to walk the perimeter of the cafeteria and discuss the following questions with their group: (1) What is discrimination? (2) How have you observed discrimination? and (3) What can we do to combat discrimination?

### Strategy Steps

Use the following steps to help you implement the *Walkabout* strategy.

1. Select a topic for students to discuss and prepare three high-level questions.

2. Form groups of three or four students. Number off in the groups.

3. Provide students a handout listing the questions they should discuss and identify the area where the groups should walk. Students might walk to the end of the hallway and back, walk outside around the playground, or walk around the perimeter of the gym.

4. When students return to the classroom, ask them to work on their own to record what they learned. After a designated time, facilitate a discussion with the whole class, allowing students to raise the key points they learned.

### Variations

You can use the following variations in association with this strategy.

- For additional exercise components, have students complete stretches (such as lunges) while they walk.

- To help them gain another perspective, once students reach a certain meeting point, instruct them to switch group members for the walk back.

### Additional Content Area Examples

This section provides examples of ways you can connect this strategy to your teaching in different content areas.

- A language arts teacher assigns students to discuss the depiction and outcomes of racism in Kate Chopin's short story "Désirée's Baby." The teacher provides copies of the following questions for consideration: (1) In what ways does racism manifest in the short story? (2) What are the outcomes of racism? and (3) What appears to be Chopin's perspective regarding racism? Students walk the length of the hallway in groups of three, discussing the topic. Once the groups have all returned to the classroom, the groups record the main points they discussed.

- To review geometric shapes, a mathematics teacher assigns students in groups of three to walk around the track and discuss where they see examples of the geometric figures they've been learning. Students number off and take turns describing or even pointing out where they see examples of squares, triangles, and rectangles and how they are important in their daily lives. When students return to class, they discuss which shapes are most common and how they impact their everyday lives.

- As part of a lesson on solids and liquids, a science teacher divides students into groups and instructs them to walk the perimeter of the gym and discuss the following questions: (1) What is an example of a solid or liquid you have seen in your life? (2) What do you think makes something a solid? and (3) What makes something a liquid? For reference, students are given a copy of the questions to take on their walk.

- A social studies teacher divides students into groups and provides the following questions for discussion while walking down and back up the sidewalk: (1) What is one reason for having three levels of government? (2) What are some similarities and differences between these three levels? and (3) What are some negatives of having three levels of government?

- To begin preparing students for their fitness unit, a health teacher divides students into groups. Students are instructed to walk the perimeter of the gymnasium and discuss the following questions: (1) How can exercise improve my overall health? (2) How do you exercise outside of school? and (3) What new sports would you like to learn?

### Differentiated Options

This section provides examples of ways you can modify this strategy for students who need additional support or opportunities to extend their learning.

- To ensure all students get equal time to participate, provide each group with a timer. Secondary students could use their phones to set a timer.

- Provide students who need support with a card containing discussion stems.

## Strategy 21: Save the Last Word for Me

*Save the Last Word for Me* is an effective strategy to deepen understanding of key vocabulary or concepts. Students in groups share definitions, attributes, and examples of terms while the last person combines the ideas into a definition. This strategy provides students the opportunity to compare their ideas while also noticing misunderstandings.

### CLASSROOM EXAMPLE

A science teacher distributes a stack of cards about cell biology and cellular processes to each group. One student draws a card, and the whole group writes down their best description of the term. Students share their definitions with the card drawer. The card drawer then takes the best ideas from the group to create a final, revised definition.

### Strategy Steps

Use the following steps to help you implement the *Save the Last Word for Me* strategy.

1. Print sets of cards with key vocabulary words or concepts on one side and the definitions on the other side.

2. Form groups of three to five students and instruct them to sit in a circle.

3. Distribute a set of cards to each group of students.

4.  Instruct one student to draw a card from the deck. Then the group members describe the word on their own paper using as much detail as possible, including a definition, examples, attributes, and so on.

5.  After students are finished writing, have the student to the right of the person who selected the card share their definition. Rotating around the circle, students provide additional information or examples about the term. As group members share, students add new information from their peer's presentation to develop a thorough description of the term.

6.  Finally, ask the student who selected the card to use all information provided by the group to refine their definition and then share it with the group. In the next turn, the next person in the circle selects a card and repeats the process.

### Variations

You can use the following variations in association with this strategy.

- Have the card drawer select the answer that was the best from the group instead of constructing a revised definition.

- Provide students with a worksheet to record their original and revised definitions.

### Additional Content Area Examples

This section provides examples of ways you can connect this strategy to your teaching in different content areas.

- While reading chapters one through five in Christopher Paul Curtis's novel *Bud, Not Buddy*, a language arts teacher prepares a set of vocabulary flash cards featuring words from the book such as *unfortunately* and *luxurious*. The teacher assigns groups of five and gives each group a set of flash cards. One student in the group draws a card from the deck while the other four students in the group write a definition for the word on their papers. Once each student writes down a definition, they share their answer.

- During the unit on algebraic thinking, a mathematics teacher gives groups of students a set of cards with terms such as *expression*, *equation*, and *variable*. A student draws a card, and everyone writes a description of the term and an example. The person to the right reads their definition and example. The rest of the group shares additional information so that the person who drew the card can refine their definition for the group.

- A science teacher creates sets of cards that have different vocabulary words from their unit about food webs in ecosystems. Each group of students receives a deck of cards. One student draws a card from the deck, and the other students in the group describe that word on their own paper. Then, students share their definitions and choose the best one in the group to share with the class as a final, revised definition.

- When teaching microeconomics, a social studies teacher assigns students to review vocabulary words such as *monopolistic competition*, *oligopoly*, and *monopoly*. Students take turns drawing the cards and sharing their answers while revising their definitions.

- A teacher of Arabic language distributes cards with different greetings to each group. One student draws a card and reads the greeting. Each person writes what they believe would be the English translation. Students share their interpretations, and the card drawer selects the best translation.

### Differentiated Options

This section provides examples of ways you can modify this strategy for students who need additional support or opportunities to extend their learning.

- Invite students to display their final definitions as a word wall product to be shared with the whole class, adding visual and artistic creativity.

- Distribute a graphic organizer so students can record their initial and final definitions.

- In advance, request that students select words from the text that are confusing or difficult. Post the words on a digital or physical board and have students vote on the ten words their group will use for the activity.

## Strategy 22: Philosophical Chairs

*Philosophical Chairs* allows students to refine their thinking in the context of a small group before sharing with the whole class. It also allows students adequate time to develop responses to high-level questions.

. . . . . . . . . . . . . . . . . . . . . . . . . . . . . . . . . . . . . .
## CLASSROOM EXAMPLE

In a mathematics class, the teacher displays a graph and poses statements about the graph. Students who agree that the conclusion is correct based on the data move to the left side of the room; those disagreeing move to the right side. In small groups, students discuss their reasoning. The teacher invites several students to share their logic with the whole class.

. . . . . . . . . . . . . . . . . . . . . . . . . . . . . . . . . . . . . .

### Strategy Steps

Use the following steps to help you implement the *Philosophical Chairs* strategy.

1. Devise subjective statements that cover desired content. Create statements that are not correct or incorrect, but rather ones that students can support or refute with evidence.

2. Establish which side of the room indicates agreement and disagreement.

3. Announce the statement to the class, and give students time to think about the statement before moving to the side of the room aligned to their agreement or disagreement.

4. Instruct students to form groups no larger than four to discuss their reasoning.

5. Invite several students to share their thinking with the class.

6. Repeat the steps as needed to address all the statements.

### Variations

You can use the following variations in association with this strategy.

- Use true or false questions instead of agree or disagree.

- Offer a continuum of choices such as *strongly agree*, *agree*, *disagree*, and *strongly disagree*.

- Give students multiple choices (A, B, C, or D), with the students then getting up and moving to the corner of the room assigned to the letter choice they believe is correct.

- Allow students to debate their choices. Someone on one side explains their case, then choose another student from the opposite side to refute that person's reasoning, continuing until all arguments and evidence are presented. After a few rounds, students decide if they would switch their position on the topic.

### Additional Content Area Examples

This section provides examples of ways you can connect this strategy to your teaching in different content areas.

- A language arts teacher guides students to grade an essay on grammar using a rubric. After deciding on a rubric rating, students move to the corner of the room assigned to the rubric level and provide evidence from the essay to support their stance.

- A mathematics teacher presents students with various methods for solving different types of problems. Students move to the side of the room designated for the method they prefer. Some statements include: (1) When solving systems of linear equations, do you prefer the graphing method, substitution method, or elimination method? (2) When solving two-step problems, do you prefer using an equation or a tape diagram? and (3) When multiplying, do you like the lattice method or the standard algorithm? Each time they choose, students form small groups to discuss why they chose the method they prefer.

- A science teacher announces statements regarding inheritance and variations of traits. Students walk to their respective sides of the room depending on whether they believe the statements to be true or false.

- After covering different early law codes, a social studies teacher reads aloud different statements to students that include some of the laws during that time period. Students move to the left side of the room if they believe the law was effective, or move to the right side of the room if it was ineffective.

- A drama teacher acts out a character's lines. Students decide if the characterization is believable, moving to one side of the room to indicate their approval and the other side to indicate the characterization could be improved in some way.

### Differentiated Options

This section provides examples of ways you can modify this strategy for students who need additional support or opportunities to extend their learning.

- Display the statements on the board for learners with auditory disabilities.

- Allow students with a slower processing speed more time to prepare to defend their answers.

## Strategy 23: Classifying Concepts

*Classifying concepts* moves the classification task from the *understand* level to the *analyze* level of Bloom's taxonomy (Anderson & Krathwohl, 2001) by asking students to cite textual evidence to support their classification. To help students with this strategy, provide a graphic organizer like the one in figure 4.3, adding columns as needed to fit your lesson.

### CLASSROOM EXAMPLE

A social studies teacher gives students cards representing various aspects of the North and South before the U.S. Civil War, related to geography, economics, population, military experience, and transportation methods. For example, one card says, "Large system of railroads to transport supplies." Groups of students classify the information based on their prior understanding and sort the cards into two groups: North and South. When groups finish classifying, the teacher invites two students from each group to post their cards under the North and South categories. Students may read an informational source or independently watch a video on their digital device about the topic. Students collect evidence to support the classification on a graphic organizer. Once the groups complete their research, they stand up and review the cards posted by all the groups. Students return to their seats and identify evidence to support their card classifications.

· · · · · · · · · · · · · · · · · · · · · · · · · · · ·

| Classifying Graphic Organizer | |
|---|---|
| **Instructions:** Read the stack of cards provided to your team. Classify each card into category *North* or *South*. Collect evidence to support your classifications and record it in the space below. | |
| **North** | **South** |
| Large system of railroads to transport supplies: | Larger food production: |
| *The graphs show many more railroads in the North and fewer in the South.* | *The maps show high food production in the South, though moving the food to soldiers was a problem.* |
| Greater population: | More trained officers: |
| *The population graph shows around 21 million people living in the Northern states and only 9 million people in the South.* | *The map shows that 7 of 8 military colleges were in the South. So, they had the advantage of strong military leadership.* |
| More industry: | Defending: |
| *The production statistics show that the Confederacy had much less capacity than the Union, with the North manufacturing 97% of firearms, 96% of railroads, 94% of cloth, 93% of pig iron, and 90% of boots and shoes.* | *In thinking about the objectives of each side, the South knew the terrain and where to attack. The Union had to invade, conquer, and occupy the South, destroying their will to fight.* |

**Figure 4.3:** Sample classifying graphic organizer.

## Strategy Steps

Use the following steps to help you implement the *Classifying Concepts* strategy.

1. Select concepts to compare and post those concept names on the classroom wall.

2. Form groups of three to five students.

3. Provide each group with a set of cards. Either label each set with a team number or use different color cards for each group.

4. Instruct groups to read one card at a time. Students decide which concept the card describes and make classification groups at their table. Once all groups are finished classifying, have groups select one person per concept to post their group's cards on the wall.

5. Provide an information source on the concepts being compared. Provide a graphic organizer for students to collect evidence on whether each item should be sorted in each category.

6. Invite groups to stand up and silently view the cards. Invite groups to return to their seats and discuss whether their cards are correctly classified or need to be adjusted. Groups discuss evidence from the informational sources to support their classifications.

7. In a whole-class discussion, invite students to share any examples of how their classifications changed based on viewing the ideas of others and their reasons for that change. If the classification is incorrect, have the group move their card to the correct category.

## Variations

You can use the following variations in association with this strategy.

- Ask groups to identify possible category names and sort their cards accordingly. In this case, each group might have different category names.

- Place category names in the four corners of the room and instruct a group representative to move to the corner where they categorized their card when they discuss the classifications as a whole class.

## Additional Content Area Examples

This section provides examples of ways you can connect this strategy to your teaching in different content areas.

- As part of their unit listening to the *Serial* podcast about Adnan Syed, who was convicted and sentenced to life in prison for the murder of his high school girlfriend, a language arts teacher leads students to review evidence for and against Syed's guilt. Students split into groups and receive information cards that contain pieces of evidence from the podcast. Groups work to classify the evidence under one of two categories: "Syed is guilty" or "Syed is innocent." They record their answers on a graphic organizer, and once they are finished, post their cards on the wall under the appropriate heading.

- At the beginning of a measurement unit, a mathematics teacher gives students cards containing different units of measure. For example, a card may read *17 milligrams* or *0.5 meters*. Students work in groups to sort the cards into what they think would be large or small quantities. Throughout the unit, students become more familiar with the sizes of units of measure and go back to their groups to refine their ideas about what measurements are large and small.

- A science teacher divides the class into groups and instructs them to read the information card that describes either mitosis or meiosis. Students then identify which one is being described and use their graphic organizer to organize their responses. Once students have gone through their cards and recorded their responses on their graphic organizer, they post their cards on the wall.

- After teaching about the five themes of geography, a social studies teacher creates cards with different examples of the themes. Students are divided into groups and classify each card under each theme.

- A Spanish language teacher creates cards with different vocabulary words learned from three categories: greetings, family names, and transportation. In groups, students read the vocabulary words on each card and determine which category each card is describing.

### Differentiated Options

This section provides examples of ways you can modify this strategy for students who need additional support or opportunities to extend their learning.

- For students who need reading support, provide scaffolding questions for the reading and closed captions for the video.

- Ask students who find it challenging to participate in class discussions to use digital tools including Jamboard, Google Slides, Padlet, or Flip to demonstrate their learning.

## Strategy 24: Chalk Talk

While student discussion is a powerful tool, it can be challenging to ensure that all students participate equally. *Chalk Talk* allows all students to participate by having students write in a shared space. Students respond to a prompt silently and simultaneously by writing their thoughts on chart paper. Teachers can use chalk boards, chart paper, dry-erase boards, or other shared writing spaces for this activity.

### CLASSROOM EXAMPLE

A social studies teacher posts the prompt: "Rules are always important." In groups, students silently record their ideas and questions about the statement on chart paper. The teacher uses this opening activity to capture students' interest and transition to a discussion on the purpose of laws.

### Strategy Steps

Use the following steps to help you implement the *Chalk Talk* strategy.

1. Identify a broad question that sparks students' thinking. This strategy could be used at the beginning of lesson to hook students' interest.

2. Post chart paper around the room for each group.

3. Assign students to groups and to a piece of chart paper. Give each person in the group a different color marker.

4. Instruct students to record ideas, thoughts, and questions about the topic onto the chart paper without talking.

5. As students rotate to the next station, have them read responses by other students and make connections by recording their own ideas or adding a question. After the activity, groups should look for themes and patterns in the ideas posted.

### Variations

You can use the following variations in association with this strategy.

- Instead of writing on other groups' chart paper, instruct students to add sticky notes with their connections or questions.

- Ask students to draw a star by important ideas and a question mark by something they believe needs more explanation.

- Give each group a dry-erase board to record their ideas.

### Additional Content Area Examples

This section provides examples of ways you can connect this strategy to your teaching in different content areas.

- Before reading "The Yellow Wallpaper" by Charlotte Perkins Gilman, a language arts teacher prepares chart papers with questions such as "What are the traditional gender roles of men and women in relationships?" or "Should one always listen to medical advice provided by doctors?" The teacher posts the chart papers around the room and assigns a group of students to each. Each student in the group receives a different color marker and simultaneously records their thoughts.

- A mathematics teacher sets up a station for students to try two lemonade recipes and decide which tastes better. Students silently record their ideas on chart paper in their own color. They also read others' responses and connect to their ideas. Finally, groups review the recipes with measurements of each ingredient to evaluate how to make the lemonade taste better.

- A science teacher tasks students with reading a scenario describing a mixture of two substances and recording their reasoning on whether it's a mixture. Students explain their answers and write questions to clarify anything they don't understand.

- A social studies teacher asks students in groups to read a prompt about industrialization between the 19th and 20th centuries. Groups record thoughts and questions on chart paper. Then, they read responses from their peers and connect these ideas to industrialization in today's world.

- A music teacher plays students in groups a selection of music and asks them who the composer is and what time period it comes from. Groups write down their thoughts and questions on the chart paper. Then, they read the responses from their peers and connect ideas.

### Differentiated Options

This section provides examples of ways you can modify this strategy for students who need additional support or opportunities to extend their learning.

- To provide writing support, allow students to use words, symbols, and pictures to represent their ideas.

- To extend the activity, have students rank ideas by choosing the one that resonates with them either individually or as a group.

## Discussion Questions

As you reflect on this chapter, consider the following five questions.

1. What are the benefits of group conversations as opposed to partner conversations?

2. Which of the strategies profiled in the chapter do you plan to use in your classroom within the next month?

3. How would you adapt one of the strategies profiled to meet the needs of the students in your classroom?

4. Which group strategy would be an asset in your classroom and why?

5. Which content area example gave you an idea for something you can do in your classroom?

## Action Steps

Use the following three activities to put this chapter's concepts to work in your own classroom.

1. Select one of the strategies profiled. Do you need to adapt it in any way for your classroom? Implement the strategy and reflect on ways to improve next time.

2. Talk with a colleague about strategies that they use that work effectively with groups. How can you adapt their ideas to meet the needs of students in your classroom?

3. Observe another teacher who uses groups effectively. What group strategies does this teacher use? How can you adapt their ideas to meet the needs of students in your classroom?

# CHAPTER 5

# Moving With Games

*Ms. Reed's mathematics class has been learning how to determine the measures of central tendency and variability. To review their previous lesson, Ms. Reed gives each student a playing card and instructs them to find a partner with the same card and stand back-to-back, with one student facing the projector screen. Ms. Reed explains that in just a few minutes, she will project words on the screen. The student facing the screen gives their partner clues to help guess the word on the screen, which might include definitions or examples. Partners repeat this process until they have guessed all the words correctly. Then partners face each other and share a high five.*

What do you notice about this snapshot of Ms. Reed's class? Is this similar to or different from your experiences with games in the classroom?

Games are perhaps one of the most well-known and consistently used methods for engaging students. Jean Piaget (1962) and Lev Vygotsky (1978) originated the study of play and games and their connection to learning. Vygotsky (1978) notes that play, often occurring with games, develops cognitive, social, and emotional skills. Piaget (1962) contends that at the third level of cognitive development, the *concrete operational stage*, students access more logical thinking through hands-on games. He notes that rules in games are extremely effective learning tools for helping students develop logical thinking at this stage. Mark Prensky (2007) contends that one of the greatest challenges for educators is ensuring Net Generation students are motivated and focused on learning due to the wealth

of technology. He further states that young students mostly learn through play, games, and gaming activities. Games can be an effective tool for helping students stay engaged and master the content. From online role-playing games to commercial simulations, gaming has become a popular teaching strategy. However, there are many ways to incorporate games into the classroom, even without technology.

Non-digital game-based learning instructs players about a specific subject by introducing or reinforcing concepts or skills or impacting players' attitudes (Naik, 2014). Non-digital games are highly customizable, which enables teachers to adapt them to align with intended instructional goals. Games can be competitive, with players trying to obtain a goal, or more cooperative, with players helping each other to reach the same goal.

In this chapter, I explore the benefits of integrating games as well as steps you can take in advance to prepare students for game-based activities. Finally, I offer twelve strategies for incorporating movement through games to boost student engagement.

## Benefits of Working With Games

Non-digital game-based learning has many academic benefits when it includes a clear educational and pedagogical foundation. Games can bolster learning as students master content. A meta-analysis examining many studies of students reveals that using academic games increases achievement scores by 20 percent (Haystead

& Marzano, 2009). Games increase students' curiosity and interest, producing more enthusiastic, competitive, and engaged learners.

Several studies have shown positive academic gains as students engage in active learning and enjoy the learning process. A 2020 study reports that primary school students' understanding of mathematic concepts improves with game-based learning compared to traditional teaching; it also reports increased student attention, interaction, and performance (Vitoria, Ariska, Farha, & Fauzi, 2020). Game-based learning includes many unique elements such as challenges, immediate feedback, collaboration, competition, rewards, and low risk of failure (Ke, Xie, & Xie, 2015). It is important though that teachers select high-level questions to maximize cognitive engagement. When motivated and engaged, even the most indifferent student is encouraged to participate in games. Educators using games can balance the need for learning, challenge, and student satisfaction (Kara-Soteriou, 2010).

Well-developed games that include cognitively engaging questions and high levels of student engagement have educational and pedagogical value. Through student-centered learning games, students think, learn, and use problem-solving strategies. Susan El-Shamy (2001) states that "Games enhance repetition, reinforcement, retention and transference" (p. 10). Tânia Gastão Saliés (2002) also documents the advantages of using gameplay in the classroom, which include improved memory, academic performance, and learning transfer, as well as social benefits. In addition, games offer students opportunities to plan strategies and solve problems without teacher support (Park & Lee, 2017).

Using classroom games offers opportunities for students to improve their soft skills as they collaborate, empathize, and demonstrate flexibility. During gameplay, students work as a team toward a common goal, creating an interdependent relationship. Players learn from each other as they listen to their teammates' ideas and different rationales for their answers. In addition, when teammates validate their answers and depend on each other in the game, students' self-esteem rises.

Teachers also benefit from bringing games into the classroom because games can serve as a formative assessment to inform instruction. During games, teachers can collect anecdotal evidence of student learning as well as observe students' social skills. This can provide information on what content needs to be reinforced as well as what individual or class skills are needed for effective collaborative experiences.

## Steps to Prepare for Games

While games can be fun for students, they should be purposeful and connected to content students are learning. Select games where you can meet your educational goals, engage students' diverse needs, and embed high-level thinking skills.

When preparing to use games as an instructional strategy, consider these key points (Talak-Kiryk, 2010).

- **Establish a clear learning purpose:** How is the game connected to the lesson objective and enhancing student learning? Games should be used purposefully to address both student needs and lesson objectives.

- **Assign students to teams:** With competitive games, making fair teams is important. Teachers must consider students' personalities and abilities when establishing teams.

- **Clearly state all procedures and rules:** Game rules can be posted so all students understand the parameters of the game.

- **Be consistent and fair:** If student answers are timed, make sure all students are timed equally.

- **Establish a positive classroom environment:** While games can energize students, classroom rules and procedures should be explicitly taught and upheld. Unacceptable behavior such as name-calling or denigrating others should not be allowed.

Many new teachers feel the need to give the winning team an award in the form of a homework pass, bonus points, or stickers. However, consider that playing the game can be its own reward. It's fine to reward the winning team, but it's not necessary. Other positive ways to reward the winning team are by writing their name on the board, encouraging the class to clap for them, or allowing them to be the first in line. In my secondary class, I often allowed the winning team to be the first to leave class when the bell rings. Students like this because it means they're first to meet up with their friends in the hallway.

The rest of this chapter describes twelve games that include high levels of student engagement and movement as students learn academic content. While some classroom games include just a few students participating at a time, these games involve all students in the learning process to reach higher levels of classroom engagement.

## Strategy 25: Two Truths and a Lie

*Two Truths and a Lie* allows students to practice finding the misconception among several options in a game-based format. This is good preparation for answering multiple-choice questions that appear on standardized tests, which task students with identifying the correct answer.

. . . . . . . . . . . . . . . . . . . . . . . . . . . . . . . . . . .

### CLASSROOM EXAMPLE

A social studies teacher explains that students are going to play a game, *Two Truths and a Lie*. Students should try to figure out which of the statements is a lie. The teacher models the process by phrasing three statements: (1) federalism is a division of power between the three branches, (2) the legislative branch makes the laws, and (3) there is a separation of power between the three branches. Students raise their hands to show on their fingers which numbered statement is false. The teacher invites students to explain their reasoning to the class and then reveals the lie—statement one. After the teacher demonstrates the strategy, students create their own three statements with one being false. Students stand up and rotate around the room, making partners and sharing their three statements. As they share, they try to trick their partner and subsequently guess their partner's lie.

. . . . . . . . . . . . . . . . . . . . . . . . . . . . . . . . . . .

### Strategy Steps

Use the following steps to help you implement the *Two Truths and a Lie* strategy.

1. Identify two correct statements about a topic and one misunderstanding.

2. Share the three statements with the class in numerical order. Have students use their fingers to show their vote on which statement is the lie.

3. Invite students to share their reasoning for selecting each statement.

4. After revealing the lie, if students incorrectly selected the wrong statement, ask students for explanations why the misunderstanding statement is false.

5. Ask students to develop two other statements and one possible misunderstanding about the topic.

6. Explain the rules of the game. Students will stand up and walk around the class to find a partner. One of the partners should share their three statements and allow the other partner to try to guess the lie. Each partner interaction has two points. If the partner guesses the lie, the partner scores a point. If a partner does not guess correctly, the sharer posing the statements scores a point and explains why the misunderstanding is a lie. Partners then have the opportunity to share their statements and repeat the process.

7. After both partners share their statements and guess, have the two students seek new partners and repeat step 6, keeping track of their points.

8. After five minutes, declare the student with the most points the winner.

### Variations

You can use the following variations in association with this strategy.

- Use this strategy at the end of a lesson to review key points or at the beginning of a lesson to review ideas from a previous lesson or assigned reading.

- Ask students to share their ideas aloud with the entire class (rather than moving around the classroom), and have classmates vote for the lie by standing up or using their fingers to indicate which numbered statement is false.

- For students in primary grades, play *Two Truths and a Trick* to avoid confusion about the concept of lying. To simplify the game for younger students, the students could create one true statement and one false statement.

### Additional Content Area Examples

This section provides examples of ways you can connect this strategy to your teaching in different content areas.

- After having read the transcript for the TED Talk "The Danger of a Single Story" by Chimamanda Ngozi Adichie, students in a language arts class develop two true statements and one false statement about the text. Students pair together and take turns sharing their three statements. Partners each guess which of the three statements is false and provide reasoning for their answer.

- After teaching attributes of geometric shapes, a mathematics teacher instructs students to find a partner, then choose a shape and secretly draw it on a whiteboard. Students each write down two truths and a lie about their shape. For example, one student says: "My shape has two pairs of parallel sides," "My shape has no right angles," and "My shape has sides that are the same length." The student's partner guesses which attribute is the lie and then guesses the shape before it is revealed.

- After covering the structure and properties of matter, a science teacher instructs students to write two truths and a lie about what they learned. Students will stand up and find a partner and review each other's statements, trying to identify which is incorrect.

- After a social studies teacher reads aloud a short story about migration during the gold rush and the effect this movement had on groups of people, students record two truths about migration and one misconception. They share their statements with a partner and determine which one is a lie.

- After teaching new vocabulary words relating to family relationships, a German language teacher instructs students to write two statements in the target language using the vocabulary correctly and one statement using the vocabulary incorrectly. Students then pair up and take turns sharing their three statements, determining which is incorrect.

### Differentiated Options

This section provides examples of ways you can modify this strategy for students who need additional support or opportunities to extend their learning.

- Ask students who need additional support to work individually or with a partner to create their three statements.

- Offer students who struggle to participate in group discussions time to think about the statements by allowing them to record their statements using technology such as Flip. Students view their partner's video and record a video response explaining which statement they feel is the misunderstanding.

- Allow students who need additional support to create their two truths and a lie before class.

- Provide a list of truths and lies to choose from during class for students who need additional help.

## Strategy 26: Chart Chase

Looking for a strategy to quickly energize students and help students review? *Chart Chase* is an interactive strategy to review content as groups compete to remember as many key ideas as they can and record them in a short time span. This friendly competition also offers teachers an effective way to formatively assess students' learning.

. . . . . . . . . . . . . . . . . . . . . . . . . . . . .

### CLASSROOM EXAMPLE

After teaching a series of lessons on world geography, the teacher forms students into groups, posts pieces of chart paper on the wall, and gives each group a marker. At the teacher's signal, the groups write furiously on the paper all the key ideas learned. When the teacher calls time, each group shares its list. If a group mentions an idea other groups also listed, the other groups say "Got it," and everyone marks that idea off their lists. The group with the most original ideas wins the game.

. . . . . . . . . . . . . . . . . . . . . . . . . . . . .

### Strategy Steps

Use the following steps to help you implement the *Chart Chase* strategy.

1.  Divide students into groups of three to five people. Hang chart paper on the walls of the classroom for each group, with plenty of space between the groups.

2.  Instruct students to record key ideas or vocabulary they learned during the lesson or in the unit and set a timer for one to two minutes.

3.  Designate individual group members to share their group's list with the whole class. If other groups noted a similar idea, then all groups cross out that item on their lists.

4.  Rotate around the room until all groups share their lists.

5.  Instruct each group to count how many unique ideas each group has on its list. The group with the highest number is the winner.

### Variations

You can use the following variations in association with this strategy.

*   Use this strategy as a brainstorming technique, instructing students to record ideas for a writing piece or science experiment.

*   Ask students working in a group to individually record ideas on pieces of paper and place them in the center of the table. The group reviews all the papers submitted and ranks the options based on criteria (for example, the best solution, most creative idea).

### Additional Content Area Examples

This section provides examples of ways you can connect this strategy to your teaching in different content areas.

*   After teaching about poetry, a language arts teacher divides students into groups and instructs them to move to one of the blank pieces of paper hung around the classroom. Each group writes down everything they can remember about poetry terms.

*   A mathematics teacher gives students an expression such as $x^5$. In groups, students use what they recall about exponent rules to compile a list of as many different expressions as they can that are equivalent to $x^5$.

*   During a unit review, a science teacher forms groups and asks them to record as many characteristics of the geosphere, biosphere, hydrosphere, and atmosphere and the different ways they interact as they can. The team with the most ideas wins.

*   After reading about early world governments, a social studies teacher divides the class into groups, and asks students to quickly write down every feature they can recall that is common to the government structure.

*   After covering the rules and skills for playing volleyball, a physical education teacher groups students and instructs them to write down as much information as they can remember about the sport. As groups share their lists, groups mark off if another group states one of their ideas.

### Differentiated Options

This section provides examples of ways you can modify this strategy for students who need additional support or opportunities to extend their learning.

*   Assign roles within each team or allow the students to choose their role. For example, some of the roles could include the following: a *reporter* shares ideas with the class, a *scribe* records the group's ideas, and an *eliminator* crosses items off as they're mentioned by the other team.

*   Create groups that represent diverse abilities to support all learners.

## Strategy 27: Numbered Heads Together

*Numbered Heads Together* uses peer teaching to review concepts (Kagan et. al, 2016). Instead of classic review games where only a few students participate, this strategy engages all students as they think about the question together and prepare an answer. All students must be prepared to answer, as the teacher selects a student at random to provide the answer.

. . . . . . . . . . . . . . . . . . . . . . . . . . . . . .

## CLASSROOM EXAMPLE

A science teacher selects the ten most difficult terms for students to understand based on previous formative assessment data. The teacher prepares questions based on the terms, creates teams of six students, and has the students number off within their teams. The teacher poses the question: "How are the elements arranged into groups and periods in the modern periodic table?" Students write their ideas on paper and then stand up and discuss their answers with the team. The teacher rolls a die, with the number five as the result. All the students who were a number five record their answer to the question on a dry-erase board. The teacher invites students to raise their boards and awards points to teams for correct answers.

. . . . . . . . . . . . . . . . . . . . . . . . . . . . . .

### Strategy Steps

Use the following steps to help you implement the *Numbered Heads Together* strategy.

1. Develop questions or problems for students to answer and discuss.

2. Create groups of six students.

3. Hand out a dry-erase board and marker to each group.

4. Instruct groups to number off from one to six.

5. Ask a question or pose a problem. While some questions could be lower-level to check their basic understanding, students can also answer higher-level questions that require analysis.

6. On paper, have students individually record their answers.

7. Instruct students to stand up and discuss the answers with their group.

8. Instruct groups to sit down when they have solidified their thinking about the answer.

9. Roll a die and ask the students with the number assigned in step 4 to share their answers. Students could write them on dry-erase boards, raise response cards, show their answers with manipulatives, or if the answer is

a multiple-choice question, students could use fingers to numerically share their responses.

### Variations

You can use the following variations in association with this strategy.

- Eliminate step 6 to save time.

- Use an online spinner to randomize who is selected.

- In step 9, instead of sharing their answers with the class, have the students whose number was selected share their responses with their group. Their group then provides feedback on whether the answer is correct.

- In step 9, after students are selected, instruct those students to move to another group and share their group's answer with the new group to check its accuracy.

### Additional Content Area Examples

This section provides examples of ways you can connect this strategy to your teaching in different content areas.

- To review some of the big ideas found in *Wonder* by R. J. Palacio, a language arts teacher asks, "What does it mean to be a good friend? What kind of traits does a good friend have?" Students individually write down their answers and provide evidence and reasoning. Each group discusses their answers and comes to a consensus. Finally, the teacher randomly selects a number, and one student from each group shares the group's answer.

- To review transformations of functions, a mathematics teacher instructs students to write an equation with the parent function of $y = x^2$ and describe what transformations must take place. Then in groups, group members share their equation, and they decide if their equation has the correct parent function and a correct description of the transformation that took place.

- After reviewing the properties of different substances (soluble, insoluble, flammable, and so on), a science teacher names two substances: salt and water. Students determine whether they create a mixture. Students share with the group whether they think it is a mixture and justify their answers.

- After showing a short video about the American Revolution, a social studies teacher asks, "Were the colonists' reactions to the British policies reasonable?" Students record their ideas and justifications, citing historic evidence. In their groups, students refine their answers.

- After covering Impressionism, an art teacher asks students, "Did the impressionist artists break the rules of art? How did this change art history?" Group members share their responses, with evidence and reasoning. Group members discuss and come to a consensus about their thinking.

### Differentiated Options

This section provides examples of ways you can modify this strategy for students who need additional support or opportunities to extend their learning.

- To support all students, teachers can use heterogeneous grouping methods to promote cooperative learning.

- Allow students who need additional processing time or language support to review questions a day in advance in a resource class.

- For an additional challenge, allow students to create the questions to be used in the activity.

## Strategy 28: Swat the Answer

*Swat the Answer* enables students to collaborate with a team and review content while moving around the classroom.

. . . . . . . . . . . . . . . . . . . . . . . . . . . . . . . . .

### CLASSROOM EXAMPLE

Social studies students are learning about different inventors and their inventions. The teacher posts the names of inventors and inventions around the room and instructs a representative from each team to stand in a designated swat box. The teacher asks the representatives questions related to the inventor or invention. Each team helps their fly swatter find the correct answer posted on the wall; the first representative to swat the correct answer wins a point.

. . . . . . . . . . . . . . . . . . . . . . . . . . . . . . . . .

### Strategy Steps

Use the following steps to help you implement the *Swat the Answer* strategy.

1. Tape off a square area in the middle of the floor, which will be the swat box. Place fly swatters for each group in the middle of the square.

2. Create questions that review concepts learned. Tape answers to each question around the room or on a wall.

3. Create teams of four to ten players.

4. Instruct teams to send one representative to be the swatter. The representative should change each round so each student gets to participate.

5. Read a question aloud. The swatters then search for the answer and hit it with a fly swatter when they find it.

6. Allow team members to help the student with the fly swatter by pointing them toward the correct answer, but they cannot touch it.

7. Award points to the first team that swats the correct answer.

8. Invite each team to send a new player to continue the game until all questions have been answered.

### Variations

You can use the following variations in association with this strategy.

- If you prefer not to use fly swatters, place answers throughout the classroom on the floor and instruct students to stomp the correct answer.

- Instead of using fly swatters, pass out flashlights, dim the lights, and instruct students to shine their light on the correct term.

### Additional Content Area Examples

This section provides examples of ways you can connect this strategy to your teaching in different content areas.

- A language arts teacher reviews important vocabulary used in Sue Monk Kidd's novel *The Secret Life of Bees*. The teacher tapes the terms around the room. As the teacher reads a definition aloud, a swatter from each team looks for the corresponding term, swatting the correct answer with the fly swatter.

- A mathematics teacher tapes different numbers around the room. The teacher calls out different categories of numbers for students to swat with a ruler. For example, students find an even number, a prime number, and a number divisible by three.

- A science teacher places images of different locations on a map around the room. The teacher asks questions about the different climate types that prompt students to swat the image with the location that best fits the climate type mentioned in the question.

- A social studies teacher poses real-world scenarios and then asks students which economics term is best demonstrated in the scenario. The students in the swat box quickly move to find the term and swat it. To score a point, the student must explain why that answer is correct. Students can choose to call on a team member for help, but they must choose a different team member each round.

- A music teacher tapes different one-measure rhythms in various time signatures around the room. The teacher claps, pats, or sings the rhythm. Students in the swat box then move to find the correct rhythm posted.

### Differentiated Options

This section provides examples of ways you can modify this strategy for students who need additional support or opportunities to extend their learning.

- Prepare questions ahead of time for students who struggle to keep pace during class activities.

- Allow students who need academic support to review the questions ahead of time with a support teacher. Write the questions in a different color or different font to support students in finding their answers during the game.

- Provide translations underneath the English answers for English learners.

## Strategy 29: No Name Game

In *No Name Game,* students are able to move, answer questions, and get automatic feedback on the correctness of their answer by collaborating with their team. This formative feedback helps students adjust their answers if incorrect, and also allows the teacher to identify content they need to reteach.

### CLASSROOM EXAMPLE

Students in a science class complete a unit on animal and plant adaptations and prepare for their test. The teacher cuts apart pieces of paper with numbered review questions and places the question slips into a bucket with a matching number. A student representative from each group retrieves a question slip from the team's first bucket. Once the question is answered, the student returns to have the answer checked by the teacher. If the answer is correct, the student chooses a question from the next numbered bucket. If the student has the question incorrect, they go back to their seat and work with their team to try the question again.

### Strategy Steps

Use the following steps to help you implement the *No Name Game* strategy.

1. Create a numbered list of review questions.

2. Cut apart all the questions and place them in a bucket matching the numbered question.

3. Divide students into small teams and instruct one student from each team to come to the front table and retrieve a question from the first bucket. These students write their name on the slip and return to their team. Teams collaborate to answer the question and record their answer on the slip of paper.

4. Students bring their answer to the teacher. Students who bring up correct answers place them back in the corresponding bucket and select a strip from the next numbered bucket. Students who return incorrect answers return to their seats and try to answer it correctly again. If they are incorrect the second time,

the teacher should provide hints and support to help the student arrive at the answer.

5. After students have completed the questions, randomly select a few question cards from the buckets or cups to designate a winner.

### Variations

You can use the following variations in association with this strategy.

- Place question cards in the center of a group's table. One student draws the card, and the person to that student's right answers the question. Repeat the process, moving clockwise around the group until all question cards are answered.

- To add a more competitive component, the students could work in small groups with the teacher presenting the questions one at a time. If the group answers the question correctly, it chooses a card in the bucket that will be the next question for the class. The cards in the bucket will have different numbers of points. Once all the questions are asked, the points will be added to see which group has the most points.

### Additional Content Area Examples

This section provides examples of ways you can connect this strategy to your teaching in different content areas.

- A language arts teacher poses questions to students about grammar. Students work with their team to determine the grammar mistake and then retrieve a new question.

- A mathematics teacher writes two-step equations on slips of paper for students to solve. Students solve the equation and bring it to the teacher to have their work checked. If they solve it correctly without a calculator, they put a check mark on their slip for a bonus prize. If they choose to use their calculator to solve it, they still return the slip, but they do not get the check mark. Students whose work is incorrect or not shown may go back to their seat to work it out again, but they must wait at least thirty seconds before getting it checked again.

- A science teacher writes examples of different scenarios that include the frequency, wavelength, or speed of waves on different slips of paper. In each scenario, one of these factors is missing, and students must use equations they learned in class to find this missing factor. For example, a teacher writes a scenario involving a sound wave and includes its specific wavelength and frequency. Students must determine the speed of the wave. Once they agree on the answer as a group, a student would return to the teacher to get the group's work checked.

- After teaching about civil rights, a social studies teacher proposes real-world situations and asks students to identify if any rights were violated. Students must name which right was violated and defend their answer with proof from court cases decisions, the U.S. Constitution, or other pertinent evidence.

- After studying kitchen safety in a family and consumer science class, students examine different scenarios related to kitchen safety. Students work together in pairs to identify if there was a safety issue and, if so, how it could be addressed.

### Differentiated Options

This section provides examples of ways you can modify this strategy for students who need additional support or opportunities to extend their learning.

- If the questions are multiple choice, instruct students who need additional challenges to write a defense of why the answer is correct and explain the misunderstandings in the incorrect answers.

- Allow students who are easily distracted in a group setting to work individually or with a partner.

- Allow students to use their notes and review materials for additional support.

## Strategy 30: Which One Doesn't Belong

*Which One Doesn't Belong* nurtures critical thinking skills by asking students to analyze the differences between concepts. The game also engages students in peer discussion and reasoning development.

## CLASSROOM EXAMPLE

A mathematics teacher shows students four mathematics problems and asks them to identify which problem doesn't belong. Each corner of the classroom contains one of the problems, and students move to the corner corresponding with the problem they believe doesn't belong. Students form small teams in each corner and discuss why they believe that problem doesn't belong. The teacher invites students to share their thinking with the class.

### Strategy Steps

Use the following steps to help you implement the *Which One Doesn't Belong* strategy.

1. Select four terms, examples, problems, figures, diagrams, or graphs with one being unlike the others.

2. With the class, model an example by showing four different things and sharing aloud how you identified which item is different from the others.

3. Present the four options to the students and have students individually think about which option is different and record their thinking.

4. Designate each corner of the room as one of the options.

5. Invite students to move to the corner of the room that represents the unique item. If more than four people move to one corner, ask students to separate into smaller groups, no larger than four.

6. Ask groups to discuss their reasoning for their decision and add on to their written notes.

7. Invite groups to share their reasoning with the class.

### Variations

You can use the following variations in association with this strategy.

- Instruct students to work with a partner as they consider the options in step 3.

- Instead of having one item that is clearly different from the others, ask students to justify any

answer with appropriate reasoning. The team with the strongest reasoning is the winner.

### Additional Content Area Examples

This section provides examples of ways you can connect this strategy to your teaching in different content areas.

- When studying poetry, a language arts teacher displays four excerpts of poems on the board. Three use the same poetic device, while the remaining excerpt does not. The students must identify the excerpt that differs and explain what poetic device the other three excerpts have in common.

- Before a graphing unit, a mathematics teacher asks students to determine which graph is different from the others: one has a negative slope, one is nonlinear, one does not go through the origin, and one isn't very steep. The teacher lets students know that there is no wrong answer if they can explain their reasoning. Students move to the corner that represents the graph they chose. The teacher circulates and listens for the schema that students already have about graphing. One person from each group shares with the whole class why their group's graph does not belong, and the teacher highlights the terminology the student mentioned.

- A chemistry teacher displays four elements from the periodic table on the board. Students must determine which three elements have something in common. For example, they may have the same state of matter, a similar atomic weight, or the same number of electrons. Students move to the corner of the room that lists the element that is least like the other three.

- A social studies teacher projects on the board three characteristics of the early river valley civilizations' government structures and one false characteristic. Each characteristic is numbered one through four and corresponds with a corner of the room. Students individually assess the statements at their desks. Once students brainstorm, they go to the appropriate corner of the room that represents the characteristic they deem incorrect. Students then share their reasoning with their peers in the same corner.

- After learning about the characteristics of quality websites, a technology teacher instructs students to evaluate four different websites. One of them is not a high-quality website. Students work in groups to evaluate the websites and determine which one is of lower quality.

### Differentiated Options

This section provides examples of ways you can modify this strategy for students who need additional support or opportunities to extend their learning.

- After recording their answers, instruct students to extend the learning by brainstorming another possible answer choice. In addition, they could create four choices for another round of the game.

- For students who need language support, post a visual representation of the item alongside the written content.

## Strategy 31: Scavenger Hunt

*Scavenger Hunt* is a fun way to get students moving, collaborating with peers, using critical thinking to solve clues, and practicing recall to answer questions related to content from a recent lesson or unit of study.

. . . . . . . . . . . . . . . . . . . . . . . . . . . . . . . .
### CLASSROOM EXAMPLE

A mathematics teacher hides ten real-world problems for students to solve in the school's front hallway, providing them with a list of clues to guide them to each question. Students work in teams to find each hidden question and solve the equation. Groups continue until they have found and solved all the equations. The group with the most correct answers is the winner.
. . . . . . . . . . . . . . . . . . . . . . . . . . . . . . . .

### Strategy Steps

Use the following steps to help you implement the *Scavenger Hunt* strategy.

1. Make a list of questions that correspond with the content of the current lesson. Hide the questions and create a list of clues students will use to find each question.

2. Divide students into teams of three or four and provide them a handout of the clues.

3. Inform students that the team that gets the most correct answers wins. Then, allow students to begin their scavenger hunt.

4. Teams solve a clue, find a hidden question, and record the correct answer on their paper.

5. Once all teams have completed the scavenger hunt, reveal the correct answers. The team with the most correct answers wins.

### Variations

You can use the following variations in association with this strategy.

- Play *Question Trails*, in which teams move from one location to the next around the room, answering multiple-choice questions. Once teams answer a multiple-choice question, the answer choice sends them to the next location. If students answer incorrectly, the location informs them to go back to the same question to reconsider their answer. If it is correct, it gives them the next question-and-answer choice.

- Set up the game outside of the classroom in the gym, on the playground, or in the hallway.

- Structure the scavenger hunt as an escape room where teams find the tools or clues they need to escape.

### Additional Content Area Examples

This section provides examples of ways you can connect this strategy to your teaching in different content areas.

- A language arts teacher places sheets of paper around the room that contain an answer and a QR code. Each QR code links to a different English or reading ACT prep question. After deciding on the correct answer, teams attempt to find the answer hidden around the room. Once the teams have found the corresponding paper, they use the QR code on that paper and complete the question, repeating the process.

- A mathematics teacher prints questions about angle relationships on paper and places the answers from the previous question at the top.

Questions should not take too long to answer so that there will not be a crowd around the most difficult ones. When teams determine the answer, they search around the room for the answer at the top of another paper, which leads them to the next question. The papers should have a symbol or letter on them so the teacher knows the correct order. When they get back to their original question, the teacher checks the order of the letters and lets them know if they have been successful or if they need to go back to a certain letter.

- Students find a card describing a scientific attribute (such as magnetic, floats, uses batteries, makes bubbles). Students work in teams to search the room to find an item that matches their attribute. Teams then record the item on their paper, draw a picture, and then search for another attribute card hidden in the room.

- A geography teacher hides pictures of different geographic landforms around the room. Teams find a picture and determine the name of the landform. Teams check the posted answer key, and if correct, they move to the next question. If they are incorrect, they must find evidence in the picture to support the correct answer.

- An art teacher hides images of six different paintings from the neoclassical period outside the school. Once teams find the paintings, they must identify at least three elements of art in the painting. Once finished, teams search for the next painting to analyze.

### Differentiated Options

This section provides examples of ways you can modify this strategy for students who need additional support or opportunities to extend their learning.

- Practice scanning QR codes with students who need additional support.

- Create heterogeneous teams to promote peer-tutoring group work.

- Provide hints for students who need additional support.

## Strategy 32: Relay Races

*Relay Races* is a great strategy for reviewing content while incorporating movement. The small teams in this activity allow for more student engagement.

### CLASSROOM EXAMPLE

In a Spanish language classroom, the teacher uses relay races in which students must translate the Spanish vocabulary word written on the board into the correct English word. The students form five teams; each team lines up, with the person in the front of the line answering one of the questions. Students who identify the English translation pass the marker to the next teammate. The team with the most correct answers wins.

### Strategy Steps

Use the following steps to help you implement the *Relay Races* strategy.

1. Gather or create content-related questions, and ensure there are enough for all students to answer at least one question.

2. Type up a numerical list of questions that includes space for students to record answers. Print a copy for each team and post them side by side on the board or one wall of the classroom.

3. Divide the students evenly into teams. Smaller teams of four to five members will give more students an opportunity to participate in the game.

4. Instruct each team to form a line across from its paper, and give the first person in each line (the team representative) a colored pen or marker.

5. Instruct team representatives to race to the paper and answer a question of their choice. After representatives answer the question, they hand off the pen to the next student in line to complete the subsequent question.

6. Check the answers to determine who has the most correct answers in the shortest amount of time.

### Variations

You can use the following variations in association with this strategy.

- Instead of having students write their answers by the typed questions, allow them to record their answers on the classroom whiteboard.

- To make it more physically challenging, place a toy basketball hoop beside the questions. After students answer a question, they can shoot for an extra point.

### Additional Content Area Examples

This section provides examples of ways you can connect this strategy to your teaching in different content areas.

- To review for a spelling test, a language arts teacher splits students into two teams. The teacher poses a word for one student from each team to spell. The students run to the whiteboard and write out the word as quickly as possible while preserving accuracy, then hand off the whiteboard marker to the next person in line. This repeats until there are no more terms to spell and each student has answered. The team with the most correct answers wins.

- To review operations with positive and negative numbers, a mathematics teacher splits the class in two and instructs them to line up for a board race. The teacher displays a question on the screen, and two students race to write their answers on the board. The student who turns around with the correct answer first wins. If neither student has the correct answer, the teacher allows them to seek help from their team. The teacher takes note of the type of problem they might need to review with a student or with the whole class.

- A science teacher divides the class into five teams and instructs them to match elements with their bond. Students race to answer until all the elements have been matched to a bond. The team that completes first with correct answers wins.

- As a review for their unit on the French Revolution, a social studies teacher gives student teams historical quotes about an event or act that

occurred during that time period. Teams must identify the event or act in a board race.

- A music teacher assigns students to work in teams and shows them a picture of a solfège note. Each student must race to the stage or front of the room and demonstrate the hand sign for the note. The first student to get it correct gets a point.

### Differentiated Options

This section provides examples of ways you can modify this strategy for students who need additional support or opportunities to extend their learning.

- Allow students who need additional support to choose which question they will answer.

- Allow students who struggle to keep pace with the class to use a timer. If they don't answer within the designated time, they may ask a teammate for assistance.

## Strategy 33: Kinesthetic Vocabulary

*Kinesthetic Vocabulary* activates students' minds and bodies as they use actions to depict terminology. Students work in small groups during this game, which promotes higher levels of engagement.

. . . . . . . . . . . . . . . . . . . . . . . . . . . . . . . .

### CLASSROOM EXAMPLE

After teaching about geometric shapes, a mathematics teacher creates groups and provides each group with a deck of cards with geometric shapes. The teacher instructs all students to stand and shares the rules. The student with the shortest hair selects a card first and acts out the word without using words. If the group members guess the word, the card goes face-up on the table. If the group cannot guess the word, the card goes back into the pile. Once all the cards are face-up, the team members sit in their seats.

. . . . . . . . . . . . . . . . . . . . . . . . . . . . . . . .

### Strategy Steps

Use the following steps to help you implement the *Kinesthetic Vocabulary* strategy.

1. Create a set of vocabulary term cards.

2. Create groups of four or five.

3. Have one student in the group stand behind a desk and draw a card. The student acts out the word. If the group guesses the word correctly, the card is placed face-up on the table. If the group does not guess the word, the card goes back into the pile. When all cards are face-up, the group sits in their seats.

### Variations

You can use the following variations in association with this strategy.

- Allow students to draw on the board or on chart paper to help explain the term.

- Have all the students sit down when one of the group members guesses the term correctly. The next person in the group draws a card. Students who have a guess stand up. This variation helps the teacher know who is participating in the game and who may need additional support or further study.

### Additional Content Area Examples

This section provides examples of ways you can connect this strategy to your teaching in different content areas.

- To review adverbs, a language arts teacher creates a deck of cards with each card containing a different adverb (for example, *quietly*, *easily*, *happily*, *quickly*, *angrily*). Students take turns acting out each adverb while the other students in the group attempt to guess the adverb.

- A mathematics teacher prints off cards with transformation vocabulary, such as *translate*, *reflect*, and *rotate*. Students take turns acting out the vocabulary.

- A science teacher instructs teams of students to take turns acting out examples of Newton's laws of motion and how forces interact with objects in motion. Groups try to guess which law is being represented in the example the student is acting out.

- To review the U.S. Bill of Rights, a social studies teacher gives each student a stack of cards; each card lists one amendment, and one student will act this out for their peers. The students who are guessing must remember which amendment their peer is acting out and state the correct

amendment number. Then, they place the card face-up on the table.

- A Spanish language teacher divides students into groups and gives each team a set of cards with foreign language vocabulary words to act out. Each student draws a card and acts out the vocabulary word, and students must guess the correct word.

### Differentiated Options

This section provides examples of ways you can modify this strategy for students who need additional support or opportunities to extend their learning.

- Create cards at different levels of complexity for different groups of students based on previously collected formative assessment data. Allow students to choose the level of complexity they feel is right for them.

- Allow students who find oral communication challenging to draw their concepts instead of acting them out.

- A support teacher may review the concepts with students who need assistance to help them adequately prepare for the game.

- For students who need language support, prepare translations on the cards for any language used in your classroom.

## Strategy 34: Pyramid Game

The *Pyramid Game* is highly interactive, allowing students to practice explaining key concepts in their own words and to receive immediate feedback from their partner.

. . . . . . . . . . . . . . . . . . . . . . . . . . . . . . . . . .
### CLASSROOM EXAMPLE

A language arts teacher places students in teams of two. One partner faces the front of the class and provides clues, and the other partner has their back to their partner and tries to guess the terms. To review the themes of literature, the teacher posts the words *Good*, *Evil*, *Love*, and *Redemption* on the screen. One partner provides clues while the other tries to identify the words based on the clues.
. . . . . . . . . . . . . . . . . . . . . . . . . . . . . . . . . .

### Strategy Steps

Use the following steps to help you implement the *Pyramid Game* strategy.

1. Identify key terminology to be reviewed.

2. Divide the students into groups of two. Partner groups should stand back-to-back, with one partner facing the front of the class and the other facing the back of the class.

3. Explain the rules of the game. The partner facing the front of the classroom gives clues to try to get their partner to state all the terms on the screen as quickly as possible. When their partner has said all the words on the screen, the guesser faces the front of the classroom and high fives their partner.

4. Post the first set of words on the board or digitally on a screen.

5. Instruct the students who can see the words to begin giving clues to their partner.

6. When the student has guessed all the words, the partners give each other a high five or fist bump and face the front of the classroom. The winning team is the one to guess the terms in the quickest amount of time.

7. After teams have finished all the words, reverse the roles so the other partner is now providing clues.

### Variations

You can use the following variations in association with this strategy.

- Use a buzzer or bell if a student giving the clues accidently says one of the key terms.

- Have one student give clues to the whole class. The teacher writes terms on paper so only the clue giver and the teacher can see them.

### Additional Content Area Examples

This section provides examples of ways you can connect this strategy to your teaching in different content areas.

- After reading *Romeo and Juliet* by William Shakespeare, a language arts teacher reviews the characters by placing students in groups of two, with one partner facing the front of the classroom and attempting to describe the characters shown on the screen as quickly as possible to their partner.

- A mathematics teacher reviews vocabulary terms at the beginning of a unit on statistics. Some of the terms include *mean, median, mode, dot plot, histogram,* and *box plot.* The teacher instructs students to describe the mathematics term using mathematics descriptions (for example, "Don't use a clue like 'not nice' to indicate 'mean'"). After each round, the teacher calls on a few students to tell the class how their partners described the word that helped them guess the term.

- As a review of the movements of molecules, a science teacher gives students vocabulary terminology that includes words like *osmosis, diffusion,* and *active transport.* Students quickly describe the characteristics of each of these terms to their partners until their partners can name the term. After they were able to successfully name all the terms for the round, students switch roles with their partners.

- Students in a social studies class review vocabulary terms during their unit on early settlement and the North American colonies. Some of the terms include *Middle Passage, Columbian exchange, triangular trade route,* and *thirteen colonies.* Students describe the words and try to get their partners to guess the terms.

- After learning about digital citizenship, a technology teacher posts key terminology including *online safety, effective communication,* and *media literacy.* Students describe the words and try to get their partners to guess the terms.

### Differentiated Options

This section provides examples of ways you can modify this strategy for students who need additional support or opportunities to extend their learning.

- Have students who need additional support form a small group instead of a partner team. Two students give clues, and two students guess.

- For students who need language support, allow them to use a digital translator app or act out or show visuals related to the words on the screen.

If they are guessing the term, students could be given a master list of all the potential terms and point to the word on the list they think is being described.

## Strategy 35: Stomp

With *Stomp*, students physically engage in reviewing key concepts, allowing them to access the embodied cognition discussed in chapter 2 (page 13). This is a great way to help students strengthen neural pathways and create sticky learning.

. . . . . . . . . . . . . . . . . . . . . . . . . . . . . . . . . . . . . .
### CLASSROOM EXAMPLE

Students have been learning about music genres. The teacher forms groups of eight students and has each group divide into two teams. The teacher places cards with the names of the music genres they have studied on the floor and instructs students to listen to a piece of music. After playing a few lines of the music, the teacher calls out a number, and the person with that number on each team stomps on the genre card as quickly as possible to win a point for their team.
. . . . . . . . . . . . . . . . . . . . . . . . . . . . . . . . . . . . . .

### Strategy Steps

Use the following steps to help you implement the *Stomp* strategy.

1.  Create cards to be placed on the floor that correspond with multiple-choice answer choices or concepts (such as mathematics properties or literary themes).

2.  Create groups of eight to ten students. Each group then divides into two teams, and the teams form lines with the cards representing the answer choices placed on the floor between the teams.

3.  Instruct teams to number off in their lines.

4.  State a question aloud or show the question on the screen, then call a number. The student with that number in each line will try to quickly stomp the answer choice. Whichever team stomps the correct answer first receives a point.

### Variations

You can use the following variations in association with this strategy.

*   Instead of standing and stomping, have students play in groups of four, with two on each team. The students whose number is called could slap the card with the correct answer.

*   Create higher-level prompts with no correct answer choice. Teams could discuss their response and then when the teacher calls a number, that person would stomp and defend their answer.

### Additional Content Area Examples

This section provides examples of ways you can connect this strategy to your teaching in different content areas.

*   After reading "Désirée's Baby" by Kate Chopin, a language arts teacher divides students into two groups and assigns each student a number. The teacher calls out a number and reads a question aloud about the short story's plot, point of view, perspective, or theme. The student with that number in each line tries to quickly stomp the answer choice. Whichever group stomps first and is correct, receives a point.

*   To review the real number system, a mathematics teacher assigns students into teams and places cards on the ground with types of numbers (*rational number, irrational number, integer, whole number,* and so on). When the teacher displays a number on the screen, a team member stomps on the classification.

*   A science teacher divides the class into their teams, with each team member numbered, lays cards A, B, C, and D on the floor, and reads off a question regarding the solar system and a list of multiple-choice options. The teacher calls out a student's number and the student stomps on the answer.

*   After teaching about separation of governmental powers, a social studies teacher divides the class into teams, with each student numbered, and creates questions that ask students to identify the branch of government—legislative, executive, or judicial—with the specific power on the card.

The teacher calls out a student's number and the student stomps on the answer.

- An art teacher places cards of different art historical periods on the floor, dividing students into teams with each member numbered. The teacher displays a piece of artwork from one of those periods, calls out a student's number, and the student stomps on the correct choice.

### Differentiated Options

This section provides examples of ways you can modify this strategy for students who need additional support or opportunities to extend their learning.

- Allow students who need additional time to think to confer with their team and then stomp, or set a timer to allow them think time before they stomp.

- If a group includes a student who is unable to stomp, designate a person to stomp for the group. That student would stomp after the selected student for the question has answered.

- Have students who are ready for higher levels of challenge justify their selection after the stomp.

## Strategy 36: Take a Guess

*Take a Guess* supports students in creating associations around key concepts in a lesson or unit. As students ask yes-or-no questions to guess a word, they create strong neural networks around these concepts, which supports the process of long-term learning.

• • • • • • • • • • • • • • • • • • • • • • • • • • • • • • • •

### CLASSROOM EXAMPLE

After learning about the scientific differences between living and nonliving things, a student in one group selects the term *metabolic reactions*. Students in the group pose questions to try to guess the word. The student who guesses the word correctly based on the clues scores a point.

• • • • • • • • • • • • • • • • • • • • • • • • • • • • • • • •

### Strategy Steps

Use the following steps to help you implement the *Take a Guess* strategy.

1.  Create a list of key vocabulary from the unit learned in the class.

2.  Form groups of four to five students.

3.  Provide instructions to the group. One person in each group selects a term from the review sheet and stands up. The student to the right of the peer who is standing asks a yes-or-no question. If the group member asks a question and the answer is yes, then the student standing shifts two steps to the right. If the answer is no, then the student standing moves two steps to the left. Rotate around the group allowing each student an equal opportunity to ask a question. Group members who identify the concept on their turn win a point.

4.  Rotate who selects the term until all concepts have been reviewed.

### Variations

You can use the following variations in association with this strategy.

- Instead of asking students to move two steps, have the student selecting the concept stand if the statement is correct and sit if it is wrong. The student could also put their hands in the air and form a *Y* to symbolize *correct* and cross their arms to make an *X* to indicate *wrong*.

- Instruct the guesser to ask open-ended questions, and the responder to give information as if they were the words. For example, if the word was *diffusion*, the questioner could ask: "Do you like going to parties?" The responder would then respond, "Absolutely! I love being around lots of people."

- Instead of having the students select the words from the review sheet, write the terms on cards on the table or projected on a screen for only the one student in each group to view.

- Instruct teams to create a graphic organizer or mind map of a concept without including the main idea on the graphic organizer or at the center of the mind map. Students then post these around the room, and groups discuss and record on their paper what they think is the key idea that is missing from the organizer or map.

### Additional Content Area Examples

This section provides examples of ways you can connect this strategy to your teaching in different content areas.

- In reviewing key vocabulary for Greek plays, such as Sophocles' *Antigone*, a language arts teacher creates a list of vocabulary words, including *tragedy*, *hubris*, *Dionysus*, and *choragus*. Students split into groups, and one student selects a term from the review list. Other members ask yes-or-no questions to try to guess the word. The student who guesses correctly scores a point.

- To review geometry concepts, a mathematics teacher gives students a list of vocabulary terms such as *line*, *point*, *ray*, *angle*, and so on. One student selects a term, and the other group members ask yes-or-no questions to attempt to guess the vocabulary term.

- To review different cell parts, like the *nucleus*, *chloroplasts*, *mitochondria*, *cell membrane*, and *cell wall* in a science class, one student in the group selects a term from the review sheet. The other group members ask yes-or-no questions to try to guess the vocabulary word.

- Students draw a card about either major landforms, climates, or ecosystems they have studied in social studies class. Group members pose yes-or-no questions to try to identify the term on the card.

- To review the elements of dance, including *body*, *action*, *space*, *time*, and *energy*, in physical education class, one student selects a term from the review list while group members ask yes-or-no questions to try to guess the word.

### Differentiated Options

This section provides examples of ways you can modify this strategy for students who need additional support or opportunities to extend their learning.

- Provide students who need additional support a list of questions to choose from. Alternatively, provide them with definitions of the words.

- Allow students to extend the learning by creating challenging clues their group can use to guess the word.

# Discussion Questions

As you reflect on this chapter, consider the following five questions.

1. What have you noticed are the benefits of using games in your classroom?

2. What other games do you use that include movement and thinking?

3. Which of the games profiled in the chapter can you use within the next month in your classroom?

4. How would you adapt one of the games profiled to meet the needs of the students in your classroom?

5. Which content area example gave you an idea for something you can do in your classroom?

# Action Steps

Use the following three activities to put this chapter's concepts to work in your own classroom.

1. Select one of the game-based strategies described in the chapter. Do you need to adapt it in any way for your classroom? Implement the strategy and reflect on ways to improve next time.

2. Talk with a colleague about games that they use in their classroom. How can you adapt your colleague's ideas to meet the needs of students in your classroom?

3. Observe another teacher who uses instructional games effectively. What games does that colleague use, and how can you adapt them to meet the needs of students in your classroom?

# CHAPTER 6

# Cementing a Culture of Engagement

*Mr. Perez prepares the classroom for the group activities. He moves desks to form discussion pods of four students, which also leaves plenty of open space for movement activities. Pods have different types of seating including standing desks, pedal desks, wobble chairs similar to stools, and pillows for sitting on the floor. Students examine the groupings posted on the outside of the teachers' door and select their type of seating preference. After completing a bell ringer question reviewing content from the previous day, Mr. Perez explains the instructional goal and introduces the activity, Small-Group Scoot.*

*In groups, students analyze quotes from a book they are reading and record their answers independently at the bottom of the sheet and fold their answers so they are not visible to the next student. When all the group members finish, they rotate seats and review different quotes and questions. This process continues until all students rotate through the four different seats.*

*Next, Mr. Perez identifies the expectations on the task.*

- *No talking during rotation, independent work only.*

- *Only move when all group members have turned down their answers on the paper.*

- *If you need help during the activity, raise your hand.*

*He reminds the class that during the last group activity they were focused and on task. Mr. Perez confidently states that he knows today will be another great learning experience. During the activity, Mr. Perez moves around the classroom and notices if any students have difficulty, then uses thought-provoking questions and hints to scaffold their understanding.*

What do you notice about how Mr. Perez engaged with his class during the activity? Do you think it created a successful learning environment? What elements stand out to you as encouraging high levels of student engagement?

By the time you reach this final chapter, you will have encountered more than thirty strategies for engaging students by integrating movement in the classroom. In fact, you will have encountered thirty-six! But ensuring student engagement is more than just implementing a handful of strategies. If teachers want to keep students invested in their learning for the long term, they must move beyond adopting strategies to the heart of the matter: they must strive to create a culture of engagement through active learning.

How can a teacher begin to shift the culture of the classroom toward engagement? After compiling decades of survey results on student engagement, Gallup finds that two survey items are closely associated to students' feelings of engagement (Hodges, 2018).

1. "My school is committed to building the strengths of each student."

2. "I have at least one teacher who makes me excited about the future."

Students who marked *strongly agree* to these statements were thirty times more likely to be engaged at school as compared with students who answered *strongly disagree*. Therefore, to establish a culture of student engagement, students need devoted educators who are passionate about student success.

With a focus on helping students succeed, how can we establish active learning environments and cognitively challenging classrooms while avoiding the patterns of students sitting for long periods in sub-optimal learning settings? Three key areas of consideration emerge: (1) classroom climate, (2) classroom design, and (3) classroom management.

# Classroom Climate

Throughout this book, I've mentioned that cultural responsiveness is key to boosting student engagement—when students see a teacher celebrating their home culture and incorporating their real-world experiences, they feel greater belonging and investment in the classroom. But cultural responsiveness goes beyond the teacher-student relationship. Committing to a culture of engagement means modeling for all students how to respect and celebrate one another, and how to make the classroom a safe place where differences are seen as assets rather than deficits.

Class cohesion is a great first step toward helping students be inclusive of their peers. In the beginning, teachers may need to assign partners, groups, and teams using the suggestions throughout the book. However, they should strive to reach the point where students are willing to partner with anyone in the class, supporting their unique needs and celebrating their differences. When all students feel included, the class culture is a comfortable and safe environment. Fortunately, using kinesthetic learning and group tasks with social interaction, as you've learned to do throughout this book, will spur a positive environment for learning as these are tasks most students enjoy.

One reason this aspect is so powerful is that it rewires the brain toward community. Working with teams and partners develops relationships that can evolve into friendships. When this happens, the brain produces serotonin, a hormone that balances mood and leads to feelings of pleasure and well-being. When emotions are integrated into the learning process, neurotransmitters materialize and raise the probability that learned content will be retained and retrieved (Herman & Nilson, 2018). The neurotransmitter dopamine is discharged in the brain when learning is stimulating and pleasurable. When students work with other students, they can become more empathetic, which also has a positive impact on their beliefs and actions in the classroom.

Creating belonging isn't just about celebrating cultural differences; it's fundamentally about creating a classroom climate of safety. Students need to feel psychologically safe when working with others. If a teacher or peer shames students who make mistakes, humiliates them for asking questions, invalidates their experiences in front of the class—just to name a few examples—the brain may interpret the experience as a threat, activating a fight-or-flight response. When a student's nervous system is activated, they may retreat or react without thinking as a protective mechanism. Here are a few considerations for building a psychologically safe classroom environment (InnerDrive, 2022).

- **Practice active listening:** Teach students to be active listeners by summarizing their partner's main points, sharing a good idea they mentioned, or asking a question. Students should not dominate or demean others.

- **Develop an open mindset:** Teach students to reflect on their mistakes and decide what they can do differently next time. Teachers can reinforce the idea that feedback offers opportunities to improve and is not just criticism.

- **Ask questions:** Encourage students to ask questions, notice their own judgments, and practice curiosity. In fact, set aside time for all students to develop a question. Students need to feel comfortable asking questions in class.

- **Create a shared identity:** Setting class goals and creating classroom rituals that bond students can develop a sense of belonging.

Consider the following special tips to enhance your classroom climate.

- Begin activities by clearly stating the activity's purpose. Make sure all classroom tasks align to standards and objectives.

- At the end of a group task, invite several students to share a compliment about their partner aloud. They also could share an idea they learned from someone else.

- Do not allow insults from any student. Should this occur, privately address the issue with the student.

- Celebrate different ideas and perspectives when they arise during class discussion. Compliment the student for posing a unique idea.

- Ensure that students aren't always partnering with the same classmate or friend by assigning pairs and groups.

- Connect the learning to students' interests whenever possible.

- Construct tasks that challenge students to employ high-level thinking skills while scaffolding for students who need additional support.

- Create structures that ensure all students participate, not just the same learners or the students who always raise their hands. Randomly call on students to share what they learned in their groups.

- Enforce the *no hogs or logs* rule with pairs, groups, and teams: no one should *hog* the conversation by talking without letting others speak, or be a *log*, refusing to contribute to the conversation. Provide talking tokens (such as playing cards or poker chips) to help ensure all students have equal airtime.

- Be intentional about building positive relationships with students by learning about students' interests and lives whether through a student survey or one-on-one conversations before or after class. Identify times for non-academic conversations or leave time for making small talk about topics important to students. These conversations can occur during classroom transitions as students enter or leave the classroom. Small talk helps students feel that their interests and identities are important (Frazin & Wischow, 2020).

# Classroom Design

The way you structure your space makes a significant impact on the learning process in the classroom. Consider how the seating should be arranged to allow students to move around the classroom and interact with peers in a safe and orderly way.

Increasingly, schools are embracing flexible spaces that enable a variety of learning experiences. This is especially relevant for supporting movement integration; as Brad Johnson and Melody Jones (2016) state, "The classroom should no longer be centered around the student desk" (p. 13). When considering classroom layouts, focus on maximizing learning instead of maximizing control. While not suitable for every classroom, consider the novel Read and Ride program, which is designed to promote movement and learning by allowing students to read books while riding on a stationary bike (Johnson & Jones, 2016). Innovative learning environments like those in the Read and Ride program challenge teachers to reconceptualize the traditional layout of the classroom.

Consider the following tips for designing your classroom with movement in mind.

- Create table pods of four desks that easily facilitate table conversations.

- Make sure there is open space so that students can easily move around and obtain materials, and so the teacher can easily view all partners, groups, and teams.

- Use movable furniture and a variety of seating options such as exercise balls, floor seating, stand-up workstations, stability ball chairs, and treadmill workstations.

- When classroom space is limited, utilize the school hallways, communal areas, or outdoor spaces for movement tasks.

Figure 6.1 (page 92) shows various seating configurations that maximize student engagement.

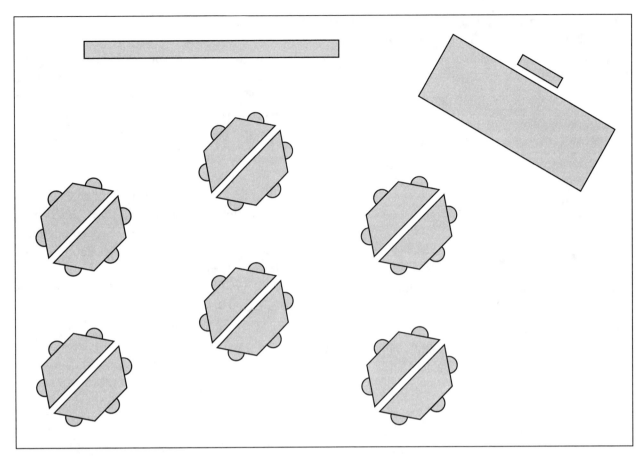

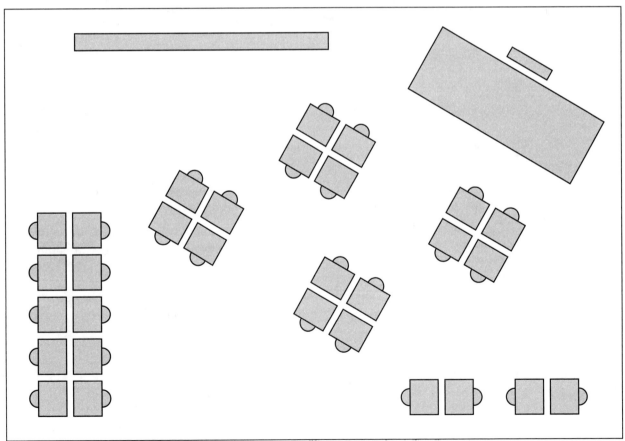

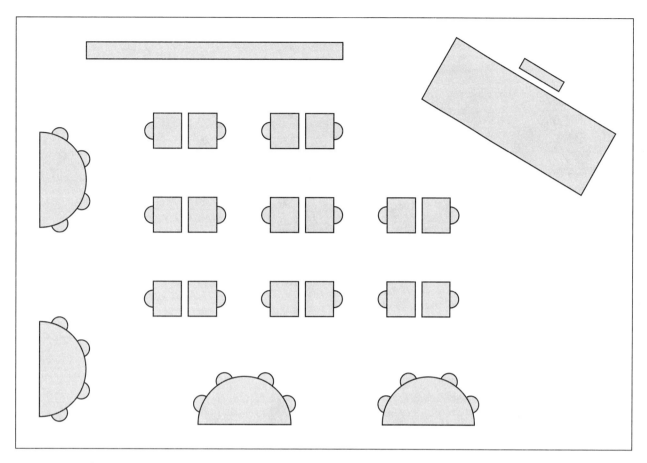

**Figure 6.1:** Classroom layout examples.

## Classroom Management

Without forethought and a stated purpose, student movement can easily devolve into chaos. Teachers often worry that introducing unique strategies will create classroom management issues such as misbehavior, immature responses, reluctance to participate, or overexcitement. Establishing clear procedures and instructions when introducing movement activities can ensure students participate in an appropriate manner. When teachers embed movement tasks, students are more likely to demonstrate on-task behavior, have increased levels of collaboration and self-confidence, engage in greater risk taking, and assume leadership roles (Griss, 2016).

Many of the strategies in this book include whole-class discussions. What can teachers do to set the tone for a successful conversation that includes the entire class? I like to think of effective class discussions like the dynamic at work in a basketball game: many players pass the ball, skillfully moving down the court toward the goal. In an effective classroom discussion, the teacher might pose a question

and one student comments, another offers supportive evidence, and yet another suggests an opposing viewpoint. Many voices chime in to contribute a variety of ideas and perspectives, raise probing questions, and make real-world connections, creating a robust discussion. Cultivating this type of discussion takes time and practice.

Figure 6.2 (page 94) examines common scenarios teachers face when facilitating whole-class discussions and provides suggestions for how to respond and an example to illustrate what it might look like. Consider using this *Talk Moves* chart to ensure your classroom discussions resemble a basketball game with multiple students contributing ideas.

Consider the following classroom management tips when planning active learning experiences.

- Consider group size. Elementary students often work better in pairs while secondary students can work in larger groups and teams. Generally, the larger the group the less time each person has to share their thoughts.

| What Happens | You Think | A Useful Move | Example of What to Say |
|---|---|---|---|
| A student gives a correct response. | *Good point! Did everyone get that?* | Get others to rephrase or repeat what was said. | • "Can anybody put that in their own words?"<br>• "Who thinks they could repeat that?" |
| | *Students heard this, but I want them to connect with this idea!* | Ask others what they think. | • "Who agrees or disagrees, and why?"<br>• "Who wants to add on to what _____ just said?"<br>• "What do you think about that idea?"<br>• "Does anyone have a different view?" |
| | *I think students got that, but I need to dig deeper into this student's thinking.* | Ask students why they think that. | • "What led you to think about it that way?"<br>• "What's the evidence you used?"<br>• "Can you explain your reasoning to us?"<br>• "How did you figure that out?" |
| A student gives a response that is incorrect, confusing, or off topic. | *We've really gotten off track. Even though they're engaged, this isn't the question we're trying to consider.* | Use your best judgment to get the student back on track. | • "Can you link this back to our question?"<br>• "Can someone tell me how this fits in with our question?"<br>• "Gee, what was our question? Let's recall where we're going." |
| | *Huh? I didn't understand that at all.* | Ask the student to say more. | • "Can you say more about that?"<br>• "Could you say that again?"<br>• "Can you give an example of what you mean?"<br>• "So, let me see if I understand. Are you saying _____?" |
| | *That's the wrong answer, and it's not going to take us anywhere!* | Use your best judgment about how to move on. | • "Can you say that again?"<br>• "Does anyone have a different view?"<br>• "Well, actually, remember when we [give correction]." |
| Students give no response, show blank faces, or offer a wrong answer worth discussing. | *That's the wrong answer, but it might be very productive to discuss it!* | Get students to say more about how or why they arrived at an answer. | • "Why do you think that?"<br>• "Say more."<br>• "What makes you say that?"<br>• "What do other people think?"<br>• "Can someone rephrase that?" |
| | *I guess they need time to think!* | Stop and have students process; give them time to think. | • "Stop and think or stop and jot."<br>• "*Then* turn-and-talk."<br>• "*Then* ask again!" |

*Source: English Learners Success Forum, n.d. This work is licensed under a Creative Commons Attribution 4.0 International License (https://creativecommons.org/licenses/by/4.0/).*

**Figure 6.2:** Talk moves.

- Establish activity directions beforehand and clarify them as needed during the activity.

- Assign student roles by letting students choose based on their strengths, having daily role rotations, or assigning roles randomly.

- Establish clear and high expectations for student work. Provide rubrics, checklists, or examples of student work so students can envision the expectations for the final product.

- Tailor the length of discussions based on students' age level. Students at the secondary level are typically able to remain focused in discussions for longer periods than students in elementary grades. One hour is the maximum amount of time suggested for students over the age of ten. Deep discussions could carry over into subsequent lessons. For students ages nine and younger, no more than thirty to forty minutes is recommended (Ostroff, 2020).

- Identify ways to transition between activities, such as asking students to return to their seats once they've finished their partner discussions. Consider playing music, counting to ten, or using a timer to support students through the transition. Students should not need more than a minute to transition (Lengel & Evans, 2019).

- Establish consequences ahead of time for misbehavior (for example, remind students to get back on task, redirect them to the assignment, provide a warning, or give them an alternate assignment).

- Set personal space boundaries. Students should move around the class without bumping into others.

- Be mindful of how you pair and group students, making sure to match them in a way that plays to their strengths and allows them opportunities to use their assets to contribute to the collaboration.

Consider the following classroom management tips when implementing active learning experiences.

- Before beginning any activity, announce classroom routines and procedures. Because each teacher has varying expectations, teachers should clarify to students acceptable voice levels, when movement is and isn't allowed, how to request assistance, and how to turn in work once completed. The class should practice these procedures with a small task to ensure students understand the procedures before attempting more complex strategies. Restate procedures before the activity starts to remind students of your expectations. If in the middle of the activity students are not following the procedure, the teacher should remind students of expectations. Showing a visual with the procedure expectations is helpful to redirect students if they aren't following the procedure. Providing clear classroom routines helps students with heightened anxiety or other mental health challenges to know what to expect.

- Use cues (such as turning the lights off for a few seconds, playing music, flashing a stop sign image on the screen, or raising your hand) to get students' attention. Teach students these cues before the activity so it's clear to students when they are supposed to stop talking and focus on the teacher.

- Positively state that you believe students will enjoy and participate in the tasks.

- Move around the room to monitor behavior and formatively assess students' understanding.

- Display a timer for all students to see and set a time limit for activity components as needed.

- Provide feedback at the end of the activity. What worked well? Reinforce positive behaviors with praise. Invite students to suggest ways to improve the activity next time. Diane Cunningham (2020) suggests teachers gain feedback from students by asking the following questions.

  - What did your group do well today?

  - What thinking skills challenged your group? Why do you think so?

  - What part of the discussion process was difficult for you? What part was easy?

  - What goal might your group set for your next discussion?

  - What aspects of group discussions are most challenging for you? Why?

  - How does sharing the thinking of others out loud help you to understand?

- • What new questions did your group raise today?

- • What might your group have done differently to improve today's discussion? Why do you think so?

- • Monitor all students as they work with peers. Do not let students merge into large groups where you cannot see them at all times. Often this can lead to off-task behaviors. Have groups spread out around the perimeter of the room.

## Discussion Questions

As you reflect on this chapter, consider the following five questions.

1. In the past, what elements have made implementing active learning experiences a challenge?

2. Which tips about classroom climate, design, and management were most helpful to you?

3. What remaining questions or uncertainties do you have about cultivating an engaging classroom environment?

4. What is your next step toward creating a positive classroom climate?

5. How will you rearrange your classroom to maximize the use of the space for integrating movement?

## Action Steps

Use the following three activities to put this chapter's concepts to work in your own classroom.

1. Choose one tip from each section about classroom climate, design, or management and make a change in your classroom.

2. If you have movement integration strategies that work for your classroom that are not in this text, share them with me and fellow readers. Post your ideas on Twitter and tag me (@RebeccaStobaugh).

3. Complete the Rate Your Understanding, Revisited reproducible, and reflect on all you've learned as a result of working through this book.

# Rate Your Understanding, Revisited

Complete the questionnaire to rate your understanding of the concepts related to student engagement and movement integration. Compare your answers to those you recorded in figure 1.1 (page 5).

| Student Engagement Questionnaire |
| --- |
| **For each question, check the box that best applies to you.** |

How would you rate your understanding of the concept of student engagement?

❑ Have not explored the concept of student engagement

❑ Partially understand the basic ideas of student engagement

❑ Understand the basic ideas of student engagement

❑ Completely understand multiple ways to engage students

How would you rate your understanding of the concept of cognitive engagement?

❑ Have not explored the concept of cognitive engagement

❑ Partially understand the basic ideas of cognitive engagement

❑ Understand the basic ideas of cognitive engagement

❑ Completely understand multiple ways to cognitively engage students

How would you rate your understanding of the concept of movement integration?

❑ Have not explored the concept of movement integration

❑ Partially understand the basic ideas of movement integration

❑ Understand the basic ideas of movement integration

❑ Completely understand multiple ways to use movement integration

# References and Resources

2018 Physical Activity Guidelines Advisory Committee. (2018). *Physical Activity Guidelines Advisory Committee scientific report*. U. S. Department of Health and Human Services. Accessed at https://health.gov/our-work/nutrition-physical-activity/physical-activity-guidelines/current-guidelines/scientific-report on August 31, 2022.

Adams, A. M. (2016). How language is embodied in bilinguals and children with specific language impairment. *Frontiers in Psychology, 7*.

Adams-Blair, H. & Oliver, G. (2011). Daily classroom movement: Physical activity integration into the classroom. *International Journal of Health, Wellness, & Society, 1*(3), 147–154.

Aguilar, M., Ahrens, R., Janowicz, P., Sheldon, K., Turner, E., & Willia, G. (2021). *2021–2022 State of Engagement Report*. GoGuardian. Accessed at https://goguardian.highspot.com/viewer/616f557ef9bf81f8cda63312?iid=617038c70db0f7943e810f0b on August 29, 2022.

Alber, R. (2013, October 31). *Five powerful questions teachers can ask their students*. Accessed at www.edutopia.org/blog/five-powerful-questions-teachers-ask-students-rebecca-alber on May 13, 2022.

Álvarez-Bueno, C., Pesce, C., Cavero-Redondo, I., Sánchez-López, M., Garrido-Miguel, M., & Martínez-Vizcaíno, V. (2017). Academic achievement and physical activity: A meta-analysis. *Pediatrics, 140*(6), e20171498.

Ampel, B. C., Muraven, M., & McNay, E. C. (2018). Mental work requires physical energy: Self-control is neither exception nor exceptional. *Frontiers in Psychology, 9*.

Anderson, L. W., & Krathwohl, D. R. (Eds.). (2001). *A taxonomy for learning, teaching, and assessing: A revision of Bloom's taxonomy of educational objectives* (Complete ed.). New York: Longman.

Anderson, M. (2021, December 6). *Six intrinsic motivators to power up your teaching*. Accessed at www.ascd.org/el/articles/6-intrinsic-motivators-to-power-up-your-teaching on May 13, 2022.

Antonetti, J., & Stice, T. (2018). *Powerful task design: Rigorous and engaging tasks to level up instruction*. Thousand Oaks, CA: Corwin.

Appleton, J. J., Christenson, S. L., & Furlong, M. J. (2008). Student engagement with school: Critical conceptual and methodological issues of the construct. *Psychology in the Schools, 45*(5), 369–386.

Blazar, D., & Pollard, C. (2022). *Challenges and tradeoffs of "good" teaching: The pursuit of multiple educational outcomes*. EdWorkingPaper: 22-591. Accessed at www.edworkingpapers.com/sites/default/files/ai22-591.pdf on August 1, 2022.

Borman, G. D., & Overman, L. T. (2004). Academic resilience in mathematics among poor and minority students. *Elementary School Journal, 104*(3), 177–195.

Boser, U., & Rosenthal, L. (2012, July 10). *Do schools challenge our students?* Center for American Progress. Accessed at www.scribd.com/document/99242229/Do-Schools-Challenge-Our-Students on July 28, 2022.

Britannica. (n.d.). Mind-body dualism. *Encyclopaedia Britannica*. Accessed at www.britannica.com/topic/mind-body-dualism on June 3, 2022.

Browning, C., Edson, A. J., Kimani, P., & Aslan-Tutak, F. (2014). Mathematical content knowledge for teaching elementary mathematics: A focus on geometry and measurement. *The Mathematics Enthusiast, 11*(2), 333–383.

Camahalan, F. M., & Ipock, A. R. (2015). Physical activity breaks and student learning: A teacher-research project. *Education, 135*(3), 291–298.

Carson, V., Hunter, S., Kuzik, N., Gray, C. E., Poitras, V. J., Chaput, J. P, et. al. (2016). Systematic review of sedentary behaviour and health indicators in school-aged children and youth: An update. *Applied Physiology, Nutrition, and Metabolism, 41*(6 Suppl 3), S240–S265.

Carson, V., Ridgers, N. D., Howard, B. J., Winkler, E. A., Healy, G. N., Owen, N., et. al (2013). Light-intensity physical activity and cardiometabolic biomarkers in US adolescents. *PloS One, 8*(8), 1–7.

Centers for Disease Control and Prevention. (2014). *Health and academic achievement.* Accessed at www.cdc.gov /healthyyouth/health_and_academics/pdf/health -academic-achievement.pdf on May 13, 2022.

Clayton, R., Thomas, C., & Smothers, J. (2015, August 5). How to do walking meetings right. *Harvard Business Review.* Accessed at https://hbr.org/2015/08/how-to-do -walking-meetings-right on May 13, 2022.

Colorado Education Initiative. (n.d.). *Take a Break! Teacher toolbox: Physical activity breaks in the secondary classroom.* Accessed at www.coloradoedinitiative.org /wp-content/uploads/2014/08/CEI-Take-a-Break -Teacher-Toolbox.pdf on June 15, 2022.

Cunningham, D. (2020). Three moves to elevate student discussion. *Educational Leadership, 15*(16), 1–5.

Dinkel, D., Schaffer, C., Snyder, K., & Lee, J. M. (2017). They just need to move: Teachers' perception of classroom physical activity breaks. *Teaching and Teacher Education, 63*, 186–195.

Donnelly, J. E., & Lambourne, K. (2011). Classroom-based physical activity, cognition, and academic achievement. *Preventive Medicine, 52*(1), S36–S42.

Egger, F., Benzing, V., Conzelmann, A., & Schmidt, M. (2019). Boost your brain, while having a break! The effects of long-term cognitively engaging physical activity breaks on children's executive functions and academic achievement. *PloS One, 14*(3), e0212482.

Egger, F., Conzelmann, A., & Schmidt, M. (2018). The effect of acute cognitively engaging physical activity breaks on children's executive functions: Too much of a good thing? *Psychology of Sport and Exercise, 36*, 178–186.

El-Shamy, S. (2001). *Training games: Everything you need to know about using games to reinforce learning.* Sterling, VA: Stylus.

English Learners Success Forum. (n.d.). *Talk Moves.* Accessed at https://assets-global.website-files.com /5b43fc97fcf4773f14ee92f3/5cca8d85fa288977b 3990a49_Talk%20Moves%20ELA.pdf on September 1, 2022.

Erwin, H. E., Abel, M. G., Beighle, A., & Beets, M. W. (2011). Promoting children's health through physically active math classes: A pilot study. *Health Promotion Practice, 12*(2), 244–251.

Erwin, H., Fedewa, A., & Ahn, S. (2012). Student academic performance outcomes of a classroom physical activity intervention: A pilot study. *International Electronic Journal of Elementary Education, 4*(3), 473–487.

Erwin, H., Fedewa, A., Beighle, A., & Ahn, S. (2012). A quantitative review of physical activity, health, and learning outcomes associated with classroom-based physical activity interventions. *Journal of Applied School Psychology, 28*(1), 14–36.

Everhart, B., Dimon, C., Stone, D., Desmond, D., & Casilio, M. (2012). The influence of daily structured physical activity on academic progress of elementary students with intellectual disabilities. *Education, 133*(2), 298–312.

Ferlazzo, L. (2020, July 24). *Eight ways to use movement in teaching & learning.* Accessed at www.edweek .org/teaching-learning/opinion-eight-ways-to-use -movement-in-teaching-learning/2020/07 on May 13, 2022.

Fisher, D., Frey, N., & Hattie, J. (2016). *Visible learning for literacy, grades K–12: Implementing the practices that work best to accelerate student learning.* Thousand Oaks, CA: Corwin.

Fisher, D., Frey, N., & Hattie, J. (2020). *The distance learning playbook, grades K–12: Teaching for engagement and impact in any setting.* Thousand Oaks, CA: Corwin.

Fisher, D., Frey, N., Quaglia, R. J., Smith, D. B., & Lande, L. L. (2018). *Engagement by design: Creating learning environments where students thrive.* Thousand Oaks, CA: Corwin.

Frazin, S., & Wischow, K. (2020). *Unlocking the power of classroom talk: Teaching kids to talk with clarity and purpose.* Portsmouth, NH: Heinemann.

Fredricks, J. A., Blumenfeld, P. C., & Paris, A. H. (2004). School engagement: Potential of the concept, state of the evidence. *Review of Educational Research, 74*(1), 59–109.

Gallup. (2014). *The state of America's schools report.* Accessed at www.gallup.com/education/269648/state-america-schools-report.aspx on June 27, 2022.

Gay, G. (2000). *Culturally responsive teaching: Theory, research, and practice.* New York: Teachers College Press.

Gay, G. (2002). Preparing for culturally responsive teaching. *Journal of Teacher Education, 53*(2), 106–116.

Gay, G. (2010). *Culturally responsive teaching: Theory, research, and practice* (2nd ed.). New York: Teacher's College Press.

Griss, S. (2016, March 30). The power of movement in teaching and learning. *Ed Week.* Accessed at www.edweek.org/teaching-learning/opinion-the-power-of-movement-in-teaching-and-learning/2013/03 on May 13, 2022.

Gupta, N., & Reeves, D. B. (2021, December 6). *The engagement illusion.* Accessed at www.ascd.org/el/articles/the-engagement-illusion on May 13, 2022.

Hall, E. M. (2007). Integration: Helping to get our kids moving and learning. *The Physical Educator, 64*(3), 123–128.

Hammond, Z. (2020). The power of protocols for equity. *Educational Leadership, 77*(7), 45–50.

Hassinger-Das, B., & Hirsh-Pasek, K. (2018). Appetite for knowledge: curiosity and children's academic achievement. *Pediatric Research, 84*(3), 323–324.

Hattie, J. (2012). *Visible learning for teachers: Maximizing impact on learning.* New York: Routledge.

Hattie, J., & Yates, G. (2014). *Visible learning and the science of how we learn.* New York: Routledge.

Haystead, M. W., & Marzano, R. J. (2009). Meta-analytic synthesis of studies conducted at Marzano Research Laboratory on instructional strategies. Accessed at https://eric.ed.gov/?id=ED538088 on May 13, 2022.

Heller, C. A. (2017). Harness fidgeting to improve focus. *Attention Magazine.* Accessed at https://chadd.org/attention-article/harness-fidgeting-to-improve-focus on August 29, 2022.

Herman, J. H. & Nilson, L. B. (2018). *Creating engaging discussions: Strategies for "avoiding crickets" in any size classroom and online.* Sterling, VA: Stylus.

Hernandez, K. M. (2018). *Activate: Deeper learning through movement, talk, and flexible classrooms.* Portland, ME: Stenhouse.

Hillman, C., Erickson, K., & Kramer, A. (2008). Be smart, exercise your heart: Exercise effects on brain and cognition. *Nature Reviews Neuroscience, 9*, 58–65.

Himmele, P., & Himmele, W. (2011). *Total participation techniques: Making every student an active learner.* Alexandria, VA: ASCD.

Hishon, K. (n.d.). *Pros and cons: Assigned groups vs. class-chosen groups.* Accessed at www.theatrefolk.com/blog/pros-and-cons-assigned-groups-vs-class-chosen-groups on June 28, 2022.

Hodges, T. (2018, October 25). School engagement is more than just talk. *Gallup.* Accessed at www.gallup.com/education/244022/school-engagement-talk.aspx on June 27, 2022.

Hoffer, W. W. (2020). *Phenomenal teaching: A guide for reflection and growth.* Portsmouth, NH: Heinemann.

Holt, E., Bartee, T., & Heelan, K. (2013). Evaluation of a policy to integrate physical activity into the school day. *Journal of Physical Activity & Health, 10*(4), 480–487.

Howard, J., Bingener, C., & Howard, T. (2021, December 6). *Essential strategies for inclusive teaching.* Accessed at www.ascd.org/el/articles/essential-strategies-for-inclusive-teaching on May 13, 2022.

InnerDrive (2022). *Psychological safety in the classroom.* Accessed at https://blog.innerdrive.co.uk/psychological-safety-in-the-classroom on May 13, 2022.

Jarrett, O. S., Maxwell, D. M., Dickerson, C., Hoge, P., Davies, G., & Yetley, A. (1998). Impact of recess on classroom behavior: Group effects and individual differences. *Journal of Educational Research, 92*(2), 121–126.

Jensen, E. (2005). *Teaching with the brain in mind* (2nd ed.). Alexandria, VA: ASCD.

Jia, X., Li, W., & Cao, L. (2019). The role of metacognitive components in creative thinking. *Frontiers in Psychology, 10*, 2404.

Johnson, B., & Jones, M. (2016). *Learning on your feet: Incorporating physical activity into the K–8 classroom.* New York: Routledge.

Kagan, S., Kagan, M., & Kagan, L. (2016). *59 Kagan structures: Proven engagement strategies.* San Clemente, CA: Kagan.

Kara-Soteriou, J. (2010). Computers in the classroom: Video games for the disengaged (and not only) students. *The NERA Journal, 45*(2), 94–101.

Ke, F., Xie, K., & Xie, Y. (2015). Game-based learning engagement: A theory- and data-driven exploration. *British Journal of Educational Technology, 47*(6), 1183–1201.

Kentucky Department of Education (2020). *Discussion: Evidence-based instructional practices #4*. Accessed at https://education.ky.gov/curriculum/standards /kyacadstand/Documents/EBIP_4_Discussion.pdf on May 13, 2022.

Kise, J. A. G. (2021). *Doable differentiation: 12 strategies to meet the needs of all learners*. Bloomington, IN: Solution Tree Press.

Knight, J. (2019). Students on the margins: How instructional coaching can increase engagement. *The Learning Professional*. Accessed at https:// learningforward.org/journal/coaching-2/students-on -the-margins on May 13, 2022.

Knight, J. K., & Wood, W. B. (2005). Teaching more by lecturing less. *Cell Biology Education, 4*(4), 298–310.

Krock, L. P., & Hartung, G. H. (1992). Influence of post-exercise activity on plasma catecholamines, blood pressure and heart rate in normal subjects. *Clinical Autonomic Research, 2*, 89–97.

Kruse, M. (n.d.). *How to engage students with musical debates* [Blog post]. Accessed at www .readingandwritinghaven.com/how-to-engage-students -with-musical-debates on May 13, 2022.

Lengel, T., & Evans, J. (2019). *The movement and technology balance: Classroom strategies for student success*. Thousand Oaks, CA: Corwin.

Lindt, S. F., & Miller, S. C. (2017). Movement and learning in elementary school. *Phi Delta Kappan, 98*(7), 34–37.

López-Bueno, R., López-Sánchez, G. F., Casajús, J. A., Calatayud, J., Tully, M. A., & Smith, L. (2021). Potential health-related behaviors for pre-school and school-aged children during COVID-19 lockdown: A narrative review. *Preventive Medicine, 143*: 106349.

Macedonia, M. (2019). Embodied learning: Why at school the mind needs the body. *Frontiers in Psychology, 10*.

Marzano, R. J. (2007). *The art and science of teaching: A comprehensive framework for effective instruction*. Alexandria, VA: ASCD.

Mavilidi, M. F., Okely, A. D., Chandler, P., & Paas, F. (2016). Infusing physical activities into the classroom: Effects on preschool children's geography learning. *Mind, Brain, and Education, 10*(4), 256–263.

McAlpin, R. (2017, April 24). Skills for a changing world: The global movement to prepare students for the 21st century. *Brookings*. Accessed at www.brookings.edu /blog/education-plus-development/2017/04/24/skills -for-a-changing-world-the-global-movement-to-prepare -students-for-the-21st-century on June 13, 2022.

McBride, C., & Duncan-Davis, B. (2021). *Ready for the workforce: Engaging strategies for teaching secondary learners employability skills*. Bloomington, IN: Solution Tree Press.

McMullen, J. M., Martin, R., Jones, J., & Murtagh, E. M. (2016). Moving to learn Ireland—Classroom teachers' experiences of movement integration. *Teaching and Teacher Education, 60*, 321–330.

Medina, J. (2008). *Brain rules: 12 principles for surviving and thriving at work, home, and school*. Seattle, WA: Pear Press.

Merriam, S. B., & Bierema, L. L. (2013). *Adult learning: Linking theory and practice*. San Francisco: Jossey-Bass.

Meserve, J. (2015, November 19). Your brain and your body are one and the same. *New York Magazine*. Accessed at www.thecut.com/2015/11/your-brain-and -body-one-and-the-same.html on June 3, 2022.

Michael, R. D., Webster, C. A., Egan, C. A., Nilges, L., Brian, A., Johnson, R., et. al. (2019). Facilitators and barriers to movement integration in elementary classrooms: A systematic review. *Research Quarterly for Exercise and Sport, 90*(2), 151–162.

Middleton, F. A., & Strick, P. L. (1994). Anatomical evidence for cerebellar and basal ganglia involvement in higher cognitive function. *Science, 266*(5184), 458–461.

Millis, B. J., & Cottell, P. G. (1998). *Cooperative learning for higher education faculty*. Phoenix, AZ: Oryx Press.

Mualem, R., Leisman, G., Zbedat, Y., Ganem, S., Mualem, O., Amaria, M, et. al. (2018). The effect of movement on cognitive performance. *Frontiers in Public Health, 6*(100).

Mullins, N. M., Michaliszyn, S. F., Kelly-Miller, N., & Groll, L. (2019). Elementary school classroom physical activity breaks: Student, teacher, and facilitator perspectives. *Advances in Physiology Education, 43*(2), 140–148.

Naik, N. (2014). Non-digital game-based learning in the teaching of mathematics in higher education. *European Conference on Games Based Learning, 2*, 431–436.

Norris, E., Shelton, N., Dunsmuir, S., Duke-Williams, O., & Stamatakis, E. (2015). Physically active lessons as physical activity and educational interventions: A systematic review of methods and results. *Preventive Medicine, 72*, 116–125.

North Carolina Department of Health and Human Services. (n.d.). *Move more North Carolina: A guide to making physical activity a part of meetings, conferences and events*. Accessed at www.eatsmartmovemorenc .com/wp-content/uploads/2019/08/ESMM _PAmeetings_lowInk.pdf on June 7, 2022.

Ostroff, W. (2020). Empowering children through dialogue and discussion. *Educational Leadership, 77*(7), 14–20.

Owen, K. B., Parker, P. D., Van Zanden, B., MacMillan, F., Astell-Burt, T., & Lonsdale, C. (2016) Physical activity and school engagement in youth: A systematic review and meta-analysis. *Educational Psychologist, 51*(2), 129–145.

Park, J., & Lee, K. (2017). Using board games to improve mathematical creativity. *International Journal of Knowledge and Learning, 12*(1), 49–58.

Paul, A. M. (2021). *The extended mind: The power of thinking outside the brain.* Boston: Mariner.

Piaget, J. (1962). *Play, dreams and imitation in childhood.* New York: Norton.

Prensky, M. (2007). *Digital game-based learning.* St. Paul, MN: Paragon House.

Pulvermüller, F. (1999). Words in the brain's language. *Behavioral and Brain Sciences, 22*(2), 253–279.

Rebora, A. (2021, December 6). *Zaretta Hammond on equity and student engagement.* Accessed at www.ascd.org/el/articles/zaretta-hammond-on-equity-and-student-engagement on May 13, 2022.

Rieber, L. P., Smith, L., & Noah, D. (1998). The value of serious play. *Educational Technology, 38*(6), 29–37.

Saliés, T. G. (2002). Simulation/gaming in the EAP writing class: Benefits and drawbacks. *Simulation & Gaming, 33*(3), 316–329.

Schlechty, P. (2011). *Engaging students: The next level of working on the work.* San Francisco: Jossey-Bass.

Schmidt, M., Egger, F., Benzing, V., Jäger, K., Conzelmann, A., Roebers, C. M., et al. (2017). Disentangling the relationship between children's motor ability, executive function and academic achievement. *PLoS One, 12*(8), e0182845.

Schmidt, M., Jäger, K., Egger. F., Roebers, C. M., & Conzelmann, A. (2015). Cognitively engaging chronic physical activity, but not aerobic exercise, affects executive functions in primary school children: A group-randomized controlled trial. *Journal of Sport and Exercise Psychology, 37*(6), 575–591.

Sousa, D. A. (2011). *How the brain learns* (4th ed.). Thousand Oaks, CA: Corwin.

Spring, J. (1995). *The intersection of cultures: Multicultural education in the United States.* New York: McGraw-Hill.

Stanfield, R. B. (2000). *The art of focused conversation: 100 ways to access group wisdom in the workplace.* Gabriola Island, British Columbia, Canada: New Society.

Stauffer, B. (2022, January 10). *What are 21st century skills?* Accessed at www.aeseducation.com/blog/what-are-21st-century-skills on June 13, 2022.

Stobaugh, R. (2019). *Fifty strategies to boost cognitive engagement: Creating a thinking culture in the classroom.* Bloomington, IN: Solution Tree Press.

Sumbera, B. (2017). Model continuation high schools: Social-cognitive factors that contribute to re-engaging at-risk students emotionally, behaviorally, and cognitively towards graduation. *Educational Leadership and Administration: Teaching and Program Development, 28,* 16–27.

Szabo-Reed, A. N., Willis, E. A., Lee, J., Hillman, C. H., Washburn, R. A., & Donnelly, J. E. (2019). The influence of classroom physical activity participation and time on task on academic achievement. *Translational Journal of the American College of Sports Medicine, 4*(12), 84–95.

Talak-Kiryk, A. (2010). *Using games in a foreign language classroom.* Accessed at https://digitalcollections.sit.edu/ipp_collection/484 on May 13, 2022.

Taras, H. (2005). Physical activity and student performance at school. *Journal of School Health, 75*(6), 214–218.

Teacher Toolkit (2021). *Tableau.* Accessed at www.theteachertoolkit.com/index.php/tool/tableau on May 13, 2022.

TeachThought (2022). *Critical thinking question stems for any content area.* Accessed at www.teachthought.com/critical-thinking/critical-thinking-stems on May 13, 2022.

TED. (2012, October). *What's good for the waistline is good for the bottom line: Toni Yancey at TEDxManhattanBeach* [Video]. YouTube. Accessed at www.youtube.com/watch?v=zJVxBrmwrYc on October 25, 2022.

TED. (2013, January 28). *Video game MODEL for motivated learning: Dr. Judy Willis at TEDxASB.* [Video]. YouTube. Accessed at www.youtube.com/watch?v=i8TPRec6OCY on October 25, 2022.

Tofade, T., Elsner, J., & Haines, S. T. (2013). Best practice strategies for effective use of questions as a teaching tool. *American Journal of Pharmaceutical Education, 77*(7), 155.

U.S. Department of Education. (2013). National Assessment of Educational Progress (NAEP) (1992–2013). *Mathematics and Reading Assessments.* Washington, DC: U.S. Department of Education.

Van der Niet, A. G., Smith, J., Scherder, E. J., Oosterlaan, J., Hartman, E., & Visscher, C. (2014). Associations between daily physical activity and executive functioning in primary school-aged children. *Journal of Science and Medicine in Sport, 18*(6), 673–677.

Vazou, S., Gavrilou, P., Mamalaki, E., Papanastasiou, A., & Sioumala, N. (2012). Does integrating physical activity in the elementary school classroom influence academic motivation? *International Journal of Sport and Exercise Psychology, 10*(4), 251–263.

Vazou, S., Long, K., Lakes, K. D., & Whalen, N. L. (2020). "Walkabouts" integrated physical activities from preschool to second grade: Feasibility and effect on classroom engagement. *Child & Youth Care Forum, 50*(1), 39–55.

Vazou, S., & Skrade, M. A. (2017). Intervention integrating physical activity with math: Math performance, perceived competence, and need satisfaction. *International Journal of Sport and Exercise Psychology, 15*(5), 508–522.

Vazou, S., Webster, C. A., Stewart, G., Candal, P., Egan, C. A., Pennell, A., et al. (2020). A systematic review and qualitative synthesis resulting in a typology of elementary classroom movement integration interventions. *Sports Medicine—Open, 6*(1).

Vitoria, L., Ariska, R., Farha, & Fauzi. (2020). Teaching mathematics using snakes and ladders game to help students understand angle measurement. *Journal of Physics: Conference Series, 1460*(1), 012005.

Vogt, M., & Echevarria, J. (2007). *99 ideas and activities for teaching English learners with the SIOP model.* New York: Pearson.

Vygotsky, L. S. (1978). *Mind in society: The development of higher psychological functions.* Cambridge, MA: Harvard University Press.

Walker, A. (1994). *Everyday use.* New Brunswick, N.J.: Rutgers University Press.

Watson, A., Timperio, A., Brown, H., Best, K., & Hesketh, K. D. (2017). Effect of classroom-based physical activity interventions on academic and physical activity outcomes: A systematic review and meta-analysis. *International Journal of Behavioral Nutrition and Physical Activity, 14*(1), 114.

Webster, C. A., Russ, L., Vazou, S., Goh, T. L., & Erwin, H. (2015). Integrating movement in academic classrooms: Understanding, applying, and advancing the knowledge base. *Obesity Reviews, 16*(8), 691–701.

Whole Child Symposium. (2016). *The engagement gap: Making each school and every classroom an all-engaging learning environment.* Alexandria, VA: ASCD. Accessed at https://files.ascd.org/staticfiles/ascd/pdf/siteASCD/wholechild/spring2016wcsreport.pdf on June 27, 2022.

Wilson, K., & Korn, J. H. (2007). Attention during lectures: Beyond ten minutes. *Teaching of Psychology, 34*(2), 85–89.

Woessner, M. N., Tacey, A., Levinger-Limor, A., Parker, A. G., Levinger, P., & Levinger, I. (2021). The evolution of technology and physical inactivity: The good, the bad, and the way forward. *Frontiers in Public Health, 9*, 655491.

# Index

### 50 Strategies to Boost Cognitive Engagement
*Rebecca Stobaugh*

Access 50 teacher-tested instructional strategies for building a classroom culture of thinking. Engage students' cognitive abilities and foster essential 21st century skills—from critical thinking and problem solving to teamwork and creativity.
**BKF894**

### Jackpot!
*Nicole Dimich, Cassandra Erkens, and Tom Schimmer*

A shift in the educator's mindset is needed to inspire student engagement and create a positive learning experience. *Jackpot!* offers immediate actions and addresses the mindset shift teachers must make to truly achieve student investment in their classrooms.
**BKF769**

### The Cardboard Classroom
*Doug Robertson and Jennifer Borgioli Binis*

How can elementary educators create a learning environment that is conducive to creativity, critical thinking, and student ownership of learning? By implementing design-minded real life examples in the classroom. All while achieving positive student learning outcomes.
**BKG023**

### Sustainable Project-Based Learning
*Brad Sever*

Learn how to design, implement, and assess engaging sustainable project-based learning (SPBL) units while ensuring students gain surface-, deep-, and transfer-level knowledge. Author Brad Sever offers a five-step process that partners academic growth with social-emotional skill development.
**BKG012**

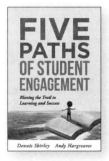

### Five Paths of Student Engagement
*Dennis Shirley and Andy Hargreaves*

This is a breakthrough book on student engagement. Join Dennis Shirley and Andy Hargreaves, two award-winning authors and leaders in their field, on a profound educational quest that will take you through exciting and challenging terrain. *Five Paths of Student Engagement* will open your eyes, heart, and mind and empower you to implement practices that lead directly to your students' well-being, learning, and success.
**BKF707**

Visit solution-tree.com or call 800.733.6786 to order.